Craniama

My Skull's Remedy

An Ethnography in Survival

Bryan D. Sisson

CRANIAMA: My Skull's Remedy
Copyright © 2022 by Bryan D. Sisson

All rights reserved. No part of this book may be reproduced or transmitted in any form or by any means, electronic or mechanical, including photocopying, recording, or by any information storage and retrieval system, without permission in writing from the copyright owner.

Any people depicted in stock imagery provided by Thinkstock are models, and such images are being used for illustrative purposes only.

Excerpt From: Dickinson, Emily. "Delphi Complete Works of Emily Dickinson." Delphi Classics, 2012-07-04. iBooks.

This material may be protected by copyright.

ISBN: Paperback: 978-1-63945-455-6
        Hardcover: 978-1-63945-457-0
        eBook: 978-1-63945-456-3

Writers' Branding Revised Date: 09/27/2022

Writers' Branding
1800-608-6550
www.writersbranding.com
orders@writersbranding.com

CONTENTS

FORWARD		V
CHAPTER 1	FIRST THINGS FIRST	 1
CHAPTER 2	NO-NONSENSE	 7
CHAPTER 3	EMERGENCE	 17
CHAPTER 4	CONSCIOUSNESS REKINDLED	 31
CHAPTER 5	CLAIMING THE AFTERLIFE	 35
CHAPTER 6	SPECIAL EFFECTS	 47
CHAPTER 7	FRUSTRATING AFFECTS	 61
CHAPTER 8	FITTING OR APT	 77
CHAPTER 9	THE FAMILY OF CHANCE	 85
CHAPTER 10	LOCATING HOLISM	 107
CHAPTER 11	WHO IS THIS PERSON?	 111
CHAPTER 12	IT REALLY WAS A MIRACLE, WHAT HAPPENED WAS JUST THIS	 121
CHAPTER 13	MINE, A TBI	 129
CHAPTER 14	COMPLICATED DRAMA	 133
CHAPTER 15	PROJECTION VS. DISCRETION	 143
CHAPTER 16	RECOVERING BRAIN	 151
CHAPTER 17	THE TABIÆS	 157
FORTHWITH		 161
APPENDIX 1	EMERGENCY TRAUMA PROTOCOL	 163
APPENDIX 2	WIELDING TABIÆS PRESENTATION #0022 *by Bryan Sisson of USA*	 169
GLOSSARY	THE A-Z OF TBI	 175
WORKS CITED	THE BIBLIOGRAPHY	 193

FORWARD

The process of actively assimilating forgotten memories can be surprisingly tedious. Even so, I find that the acquisition and order garnered from the survivor's reality pre-trauma is of paramount importance as the survivor reestablishes her/his identity within social consciousness. I have discovered so many intricacies associated with my own brain injury, that the more I wrote, the more difficult it became to perceive myself as distanced from my initial point of trauma. The truth about surviving conveys the reality of adaptation. Do not think that by reading this book or making it through the first 15 years with a head injury will completely erase the desires to surrender your shadow-self. For its in the renewing of our minds that we can thrust our shadow-selves back into the realm of consciousness. Recovery shan't be viewed as something from which survivors will, or even can for that matter, simply "heal". Submit to the process of the survivor's acquired homeostasis.

This volume is riddled with unending examples of acquired verbosity. As most survivors are aware, verbosity is the clinical term for describing occasional repetitions of ideas in verbiage. I make witness now to a personal struggle. Even though the industrious evaluators of English and writing styles may tell you that my penmanship is often filled with cliches and often clumsy in nature, I have left several areas of this publication as I wrote them when I was still inside the TABIÆS scale. Professional perceptions of my authorship are difficult for me to accept; but (and here comes my cliche!) with a disability that is hidden from view, other areas in the survivor's reality post-trauma expose the awkward truths of head-injury.

I've read several books about the ordeals experienced by survivors, and I thought I could differentiate myself by composing my ethnography in ways that would transcend the confusing negativities innate to survival of TBI. Alas, this first book covering my cranium and it's natural personality shift may not translate to the medical community as I had first hoped. But these few paragraphs on personal hopes and struggles describe the catch-22 exhibited by the community of survivors in sTBI. In some ways I have come so far, but the output of my acquired abilities will always shine brighter than that which I believe I should have portrayed.

Furthermore, I describe the person/personality before TBI as a survivor's shadow or the "shadowself". Ancient Egyptians described the personality of what they would do or would have done as a concept that was always with the individual, but seen by others as that individual's shadow. If I didn't have facial and vocal cord paralysis, I'm certain that I would be on stage somewhere or employed as a choral conductor/vocal coach. The hopes and dreams of my life pre-TBI are ever with me, but rarely seen or thought of by anyone else; you see, they are found in my shadow. If for no other reason than using this terminology while reading my book, the praxis from Ancient Egypt allows "me" to conceptualize the "me" seen by others today, and the "me" I know to be my "me".

Qualifying one's individual experience as "good," "bad," better or worse, etc. is fundamentally futile. As you read this idiography, I impassion you to realize that a larger number of brain injured survivors, often ignored and sometimes unaccounted, have experienced way worse than me. So many have died that those of us surviving might successfully manifest *craniama*. In the remembrance of those who came before and the realized perplexities of "handicap" and "disability," individuals touched by brain injury beholden all to profound, new depths in understanding the greater, human experience.

Claiming membership to this family of survival is never voluntary. Loss of Consciousness (LoC) in moderate to severe acquired brain injuries (m-sABI) changes survivors. No survivor of significant head trauma returns to a state of non-injury. Symptoms persist years after external recovery appears completed. The human body cannot recreate lost neurons; therefore, the injured brain is encumbered by the sociocultural dance of trial-and-error as survival personalities uniquely engage the rhythms to the coma catch-up.

Pulvis et umbra sumus.
"We are but dust and shadow."

—Horace

CHAPTER 1

FIRST THINGS FIRST

So many times, when I inform people I suffer TBI, they toss back with chagrin, "We *all* suffer from too much information; you're no different." A traumatic brain injury (TBI) is *not* TMI! During my recovery, I often experienced hurt feelings when misunderstandings arose from what I thought were tangible ideas that "intelligent" individuals ultimately chose to ignore. More often than not, I have witnessed what I now believe to be just natural tendencies of human behavior.

I've been tending this idiography — maintaining this journal — since returning home from the hospital at Christmas 1999. As with any *diary* that you might read, there may be stories you disagree with at times or moments you believe are described incorrectly. Its important to keep in mind that this work, *Craniama*, while meant to help others perceive severe-closed head injured survivors more accurately, the writing (of my own independent perspective) is in and of the past.

Later in this book, I present a traditional Hindu hymn, but there is a line I truly like that goes something like this, *"I feel... I have felt... that is all."* In this book when I say, I feel, this is happening;" I am actually saying, "I have felt... because to my mind's eye, such and such was happening." The great, classical anthropologists were trained to write their *ethnographies* in the present tense at the moment they encountered the experience, which is different from a diary where an author usually speaks of events in past tense.

The majority of these chapters were written ¾ of my journey through recovery (I started my note-taking around 2011). And as much of the writing is in present tense, my personal reflections do not necessarily reflect ongoing emotions towards any individuals or fleeting instances regarding natural human behavior. As with any ethnography, this is the stepping stone towards understanding a population that has no voice during their time along what I have named, the *"craniamatic"* line, in the recovery paradigm of the TABIÆS. (*Don't worry, I'll explain more fully thereinafter.*)

In life's unending lessons, a variety of counter traditions have become the preferred tutorials of a great too many. Our world has devolved into chaotic interplay in their own eyes that uplifts the offense so as to recreate the nexus of defending themselves. Appreciation for the qualitative process became mired in an overgrowth of revisions that exalted the synaposematic.

"If I can see it, then I'll believe it." To be sure, "if I can locate academic studies that address the problems and/or solutions described, then I'll allow myself invest effort within this relationship." But if I can't see it, shouldn't that mean one must subsequently find your story false?

What about the Jewish rabbi who taught that faith is being sure of what we hope for and certain of what we do not see? Conversely, the Buddha posed that the way in which theology needs faith is inversely proportional to the practice of Zen, which fundamentally requires confidence built upon tangible knowledge. As a free-thinker, will you rely only upon faith smaller than mustard seeds or might you require precise knowledge that has no other purpose than to be experienced?

Merriam Webster would inform you that *faith* is the essence of loyalty to a thing or person; fidelity to one's promises; or some sincerity of intentions. Further, what might happen if we take such an idea of "faith" *outside* religious context? *Yikes*! The secular world wants faith in nothing but the self! I was so surprised in the spring of 2011 when I gifted a faith-leaning sign to a secular youth organization. The sign was practically ripped from my hands before I could get it on the wall, and individuals governing club memberships informed me that I was no longer welcome on campus. I could hardly believe it!

When I wrote this introduction, I was still reeling from the animosity projected onto me that April Fool's Day in 2011. I had purchased a small sign for decorating in the kitchen that boldly stated, "The Recipe for Friendship:" it was something ridiculously homey like a mother might hang in her kitchen, "2 cups fresh kindness, 1 tbsp of joy, 3 sticks of laughter, melted and bubbly, 6 tsp of merriment, all baked in a bowl of trust until a wholesome, golden brown. While removing from the oven, sprinkle with faith and good cheer."

I commented with a smile that I was surprised it had said "faith" on the ingredient list, adding, "Oh, I didn't realize it said that! But I guess I have faith in you, and I think you have faith in me. No?" The decision to have me leave that youth group organization was heralded in front of a youth member to whom I was teaching piano lessons. They told me to leave immediately. This hurt my feelings very much, because I had been spending so much time helping youth and teaching piano and voice lessons.

Don't worry though, even though I'll be addressing religious treatment of disabilities shortly, my ethnography is not an argument of religious teaching, nor is it even an argument over faith! I know I was dismissed because youth, volunteers, adults, friends, and even my own family of choice, hadn't the slightest clue on how to incorporate or make provisions for my survival personality based on the acquired abilities that remained hidden even to myself until now.

I began writing my personal experience for the sole purpose of understanding myself more completely, but also as a way of formulating difficult concepts into rational words not easily grasped by family and friends. The underlying premise of this idiography is entrenched in the foundation that so many survivors, their families and friends have, are, and/or may be soon struggling with acquired differences inflicted via brain injured phenomenon. Counselors, psychologists, friends and even family at times suggest that I ought relax, calm down, join a support group or "*something*". How can a brain whose thoughts clunk together sporadically "calm down"? It's my hope that you may come to understand that the ability to calm down or be normal is a concept the survivor will lose, but through recovery they'll locate appropriation.

Our current society needs to learn that if someone says they suffered a brain injury, it is NOT hereditary nor is it contagious! I had a girl once tell me that she would not allow a romantic relationship to develop because she didn't want her children to be disabled. Our sociocultural lens has widened greatly over the past few years, but we still have so much more to accomplish. Since the individual psychology of human behavior highlights the seeking of others who are like-minded and equal to our self-perception; it's no wonder that individuals with acquired differences find themselves lost in social groups.

To find "friends" many will suggest joining a support group for ABI individuals. At this time, however, a stable network of professionals grouping survivors into cohorts where they might find inclusion is unavailable to many survivors at this time. This is not to say that such helpers are non-existent, they just require some special navigating on the world wide web or within our communities to find individual groups the most like us. Some ABIs may find the perfect network quickly, with very little effort. For others, it may take longer, but that is due to the traumatized focal point, which is experienced differently by every closed-head brain injury.

Yes, hypocrisy - which according to Dictionaire á Sissone means, "deceiving your fellow citizen for the express purpose of jumping ahead" - has taught us to not believe people when individuals claim "handicap!" crying out, "the pain is so severe!" At least, we shouldn't believe them unless their is a sign, such as a wheelchair, walking cane, trained mammal, or noticeable limp; right? It's easy to sum predominant signs of obvious handicap with one term I will use throughout this book, represented by a blue placard (BP). I'm sure you know to what I refer, the one hanging from the rearview mirror of their vehicles, which enable them to park closer than the average Joe Six-pack at any venue with handicap BP parking.

While writing this book, I've attempted to use positive and generic terms, to where we can keep from identifying individuals with TBIs as victims, patients and/or handicapped. Even though society addresses us as BP individuals, there are vast differences in our make-up. For that matter, anyone experiencing an acquired handicap after maturity is different in many cases, but for this book, I've narrowed the scope. I'm only speaking to individuals having closed-head brain injuries with loss of consciousness greater than 24 hours.

We've all come across people whom we think aren't deserving of special treatment. For example, the Mayberry High-School-aged clown who parks his teacher's car in the BP-spot at the grocery store so it will be towed for practical joke; not to mention Laye Z. Susan who had to refrain from buying much needed groceries because the BP parking spaces were full and she didn't have enough gas money to sit and wait for one to open up. How annoying is it to see someone stroll leisurely into the mall after parking with BP and watch another car park far from the door, with their wheelchair. As Stephen Colbert learned from me, "Ohhh, the injustice!"

I wrote this book to better understand myself, but found that transferable knowledge might be available to others facing hardships with their injuries and acquired differences. The underlying premise for why my experience became a book rests in the fact that so many of us have brain injuries and hidden handicaps. TBIs are not open to group therapy in my opinion. There are too many levels of recovery, too many facets of maturity to lump everyone together based on ABIs.

It's true that each person has genetic composure singular and unique, making up the individual - different hair colors, various eye-shapes, lean-to-fat ratios, gender differentials, nose sizes, and lengths of fingers - but I'll leave those measurements to someone more qualified in medicine or physical anthropology. It's also true that each of us has monolithic reasoning to attach meanings to words and communicate with those around us, but yet again such would be a book or research project designed by those we call linguists.

But what about the pain-level scale of each person? What about their emotions and/or opinions? What about the many perspectives on the make-up of the human persona? Normally, I would sit down and communicate, "Well, let's ask what others have to say." I know many others who would argue, saying, "Leave this drama to the person to figure out [on their own], it'll work out for them; my life isn't that weird." I'm glad that you've already agreed with me in this way of acquiring my book. By listening to other perspectives, we can manifest holism in comprehending our plights as survivors living with new personalities... i.e. our TBIs. So don't delay, let's have a read.

The Poet Perplext

Brain! you **must** work! begin or we shall lose
The day, while yet we only think upon it.
The hours run on and yet, you will not choose:
One subject — *come* — ode, elegy, or sonnet.
You must contribute, Brain! in this hard time;
Taxes are high, food: dear, and we must rhyme.

'T'were well as when I rubbed my itching head,
The fingers with benignant stimulation,
Could thro' its medullary substance spread,
True motions of poetic inspiration;
But *scratch*, or *knock*, even *shake* my head about,
The motions, although going, nought comes out.

The natural Mind, consider good, my Brain,
In the Mind, politic bears some daft allusion;
Limbs and Atlas *serve*, support your reign,
Along with all when thrown into confusion.
But *Caput* mine, in truth, I shan't support;
A Head so lazy as if born too long ago at court.

My verse goes on, and we shall have, dear friend;
A poem, 'ere the subject be determined.
But everything should have some useful end,
That single line itself is worth a sermon!
A moral point so obvious, is *just* as good —
Hence, my gentle Brain, I thank you now and so conclude.

— Robert Southey

CHAPTER 2

NO-NONSENSE

Before understanding fully, those willing to learn gain insight from libraries, philosophers, the wise and others more educated than themselves. I know of friends who would sit me down to explain that truest wisdom comes only from they whom have little; i.e., how can one truly understand the pangs of life if they refuse to ignore the graces of the trinity, God-head, or other religious paradigms? Regardless of all that though, the USA educational department has a range of standards within its accreditation processes, through which "We the people," might form a better Union utilizing appropriate learning.

All traumatic brain injuries involve some unnatural force that leads to the acquisition of damage to the brain. Acquired difference issues exist because forcefulness makes contact with the skull in a diverse set of scenarios. Head trauma manifests in varied levels of consciousness, comatose, and even death. For the purpose of differentiation, we must be aware that the human body post-ABI may still yet terminate in three distinct phases. In the realm of severe acquired brain injuries (sABIs), there is always a high potential in outcomes that are unfavorable. Deaths can potentially occur at three specific points in time following the trauma: immediately after the injury, within 2 hours following the injury, and the brain can remain unstable as long as three weeks following the trauma.

Brain injuries are not a new phenomenon, because they have existed as long as humans have been living on the earth. Archaeological expeditions in France have shown that opened-head brain injuries were in existence as early as 6500B.C.E. Since more recent ancient times however, a practice called 'trepanation' was developed to remove portions of the skull so that professional surgeons might access the dura matter of the brain and/or relieve intracranial pressures.

A primary aspect of most Ancient Near Eastern cultures involves a connection between health matters and deified powers, proposed to be either demonic or divine. Illnesses were seen as punishments for irregular, pre-meditated sins. Therefore, in order to be cured from an unknown illness, aside from any possibly available rational medicine, subsequent prescriptions in meditation were utilized. Respectful appeals to the healing god, goddess or demon would have to be made using methods believed to appease said spiritual forces.

The first step of the healing process was determining which sin had caused the unnatural weakness. Secondly, one had to determine which deified figure had taken offense and therefore responsible for the punishment. This deity would only have the power of redemption for the committed sin. Lastly, it would further be determined which purification rituals would be necessary to undo the illness. Due to the polytheistic nature of many Ancient Near Eastern religions, one would have to repeat this exercise until the correct deity was uncovered, if the disease persisted after performing purification rituals. If the curse was believed to have been found, a sacrifice for possible appeasement of the deity in exchange for the removal of the illness was recommended. These rituals were usually performed at a specific temple dedicated to a god or goddess and individuals would travel great distances.

In pre-modern Europe, Hippocrates gave specific instructions on trepanation, and Galen elaborated upon the procedure. Wealthy and prominent individuals were primarily the majority of individuals who could afford this procedure in ancient times. In and of itself, the procedure was used more for alleviating seizures and skull fracture healing. However, we have in history the picture of a crazy family member whom we allowed to remain aloof and socially distant because physical and cognitive therapies did not formally exist. Survivors of trepanation rarely made full recoveries, and were often, as Aristotle had suggested, "put away," in locations hidden from social consciousness. Thankfully, we live in an age where anthropological, medical and technological intelligences often freshly stimulate healing strategies.

But the word… Craniama… is that supposed to enlighten us towards some paradigm of some brainy-infused wonder-ama? Nearly two thousand years ago, the Ancient Greeks began creating suffixes, prefixes, etc. as a way to provide everything known to the Hellenistic world with a linguistically Greek descriptor. (Word lists and dictionaries are available in abundance through any online search engine of your choice.) When the ancient philosophers arrived at naming the head, they did give it the name cranium, which is in use to this day in medical communities. But its peribology; that is, its *symbolic anthropology* or *linguistic reality* is so much more.

The actual word base of my wording is built upon κρανία (crania) which specifies an ideology of a skull. At the same time, Ancient Greeks used the word κραν- (cran-) to exemplify a helmet worn in battle. The ending -ιαμα (-iama) when added to the end of a word, specified an awareness to successful treatment or examples of some appropriate remedy and/or cure. In understanding the brilliance of humanity, it is exceedingly more than pertinent to comprehend the fundamental uniqueness of every individual person. Because this is my personal experience in recovering from severe TBI, it does not mean that your experience in recovery-time will be the same as mine. Humanity is diverse, and therefore every outcome from an injury to the brain is different.

The injury this book is written toward is intended for use by survivors, their friends and families. Just as the uniqueness of individuals, the onset of trauma has a broad quotient of varying degrees in onset possibilities; although, an acquired brain injury (ABI) is always the result of some direct disruption to the brain, internally or externally applied. ABIs come in two styles. Firstly, opened-head brain injuries result when the outside force is powerful enough to puncture or crack an opening in the skull and introduce foreign elements, chemicals or objects to the dura matter. Secondly, closed-head injuries oftentimes include the side effects associated with violent shearing, that outside forces cause the brain to rotate unrestrainedly while the skull remains intact. The family of ABIs is growing. Some instances of the Long Covid have resulted in significant brain damage. Current researchers consider the still elusive and little understood Havana syndrome incurred by federal employees in certain international locations to also cause such injuries.

When closed-head brain injuries develop extraneous spinal fluid or the blood brain barrier becomes dysfunctional, a shunt punctures a small area of the skull for the purpose of drawing out the excess liquid. Chemically-induced brain injuries are most commonly due to over production of bodily hormones and/or fluids. The shunt must be employed for quickened release of dangerous pressurization risks happening within the skull. Quite often, a reputably painful procedure called the spinal tap will also be prescribed by physicians in order to fully eliminate the production. Overall, these injuries are then styled as opened-head brain injuries.

In most cases, open/ed-head brain injuries tend to have preferential outcomes when compared with their closed-head counterparts, in my opinion, because medical researchers have been perfecting trepanation for centuries. Medical professionals have come so far in successfully helping patients adapt to their personalities now with acquired differences.

According to a medscape publication, the financial costs of traumatic brain injuries on the US population sum to a total of nearly $100 billion per year. The article goes on to explain that while a steep, 36% of severe TBIs result in death; approximately 2,500 individuals are handicapped each year due to a subsequent, persistent vegetative state.

The National Institute of Neurological Disorders and Stroke defines TBI as a "form of acquired brain injury, [through which] some sudden trauma causes damage to the brain." As previously stated, TBIs always result from some impacting force. These forces include, but are not limited to: open head injury, closed head injury, deceleration injury, chemical/toxic, hypoxia, tumor, infection or stroke.

Opened-head ABIs comprise any number of sharp objects that can puncture and/or damage the skull, thus exposing the brain to unnatural materials with direct access to nature's elements and human-made objects. As stated above, physicians have been toying with trepanation for centuries. Even so, as most anatomical progressions of understanding are phenomenal within society, the more superior medical communities have made brilliant strides in adapting technology towards healing purposes. Such developments aid in awareness to necessary precautions and acceptable procedures for returning the skull, brain and even the survivor's original personality to a repaired, normative state. Normalcy is best achieved by utilizing aggressive re-adaptation in the realm of physical movement, diverse therapies, tireless social exposure and making allowances for an unprecedented aptitude for sociocultural mistakes.

Despite the broad location of brain injury, i.e. the human head; the uniqueness of an individual's interaction with their world portrays the endless amount of possibilities which can potentially cause an individual to acquire a brain injury. According to the TBI Recovery Center there are just over one million cases of ABIs reported each year inside the USA alone. Overall, however, a total of 80% of these cases are identified as mild brain injuries (mABIs).

Since embarrassment, shame and even animosity can likely affect survivors, there is a propensity for individuals to not report hitting the head or getting punched or acquiring a concussion. The stigma of handicaps is rather shocking. So many individuals throughout the world despise social judgments and will go out of their way to avoid being labeled if at all possible.

Brain injuries caused by motor vehicle accidents rank highest of severe brain injury causes, totaling 45% of ABI cases. ABIs caused from physical assaults make the next to largest cohort, ranking at 30% of the national average in a given year. Sadly, over three-hundred infants' lives are terminated in the USA because of caregivers who violently shake their babes. Twelve-to-fifteen-hundred tiny humans experience the terrifying symptoms of the shaken baby.

Overall, there are an estimated 1.7 million ABIs each year according to the US Center for Disease Control (CDC). Additionally, 75-80% of these acquired differences are concussions or moderate head injuries. This means that a bewildering 425,000 individuals experience debilitating or deadly ABIs each year. Surprisingly, the place that has the opportunity to portray the actual ordeal of survival the best often glosses - with a greater than 90% production rate - over the individual struggles and arduous disappointments encountered by the presence of a brain injury.

When people go to the movies, the goal is to have fun. For those of us who get hit by high-end action movies, media evaluators and film critics would give a significantly low rating to an action-packed movie where the protagonist ends up in a coma after a closed head injury and remains in a coma until the end of the movie. Or perhaps the patient can wake up from a coma having slept through therapy, remembering, and returning to work in the Senior Year. In my opinion, the reason for this is other than entertainment value.

Remembering that closed-head brain injuries often remain unreported, grasping an abstract idea that a traumatic experience, such as the shaking of a head, could seriously result in physical differences, injuries, or even death remains too "unbelievable" for the general public. Regrettably, brain injuries are often too difficult to understand by others who do not live day-to-day with the traumatic affects. Additionally, I have heard that many sABIs never progress to a level that is purely undetectable by others.

I'd like to take a moment to just extend my sympathy to you if your survivor is not awakened. In my home state of Texas, just a few weeks ago, a Hispanic mother of two girls was in an accident and lying in a comatose. Her wish was to never be a burden to her family by requiring hospital bills and life support. However, the States hands were tied and physicians would not disconnect her as per her instructions for one very precious reason. The woman was 7.5 months pregnant. Just remember that no matter what an individual may say pre-trauma, extending the possibility of life is better than deciding death could be better. I'm not referencing any support or dissension to abortion… I'm talking about the mother in this scenario. The likelihood that you may be presented with deciding between two unfavorable outcomes may lead you to just wash your hands of the situation. Conquer your own emotions and trust in life.

When phrasing the, "second birth," I merely am describing the reawakening to life from comatose. For milder traumatic experiences when no comatose is present, the moment memorable consciousness is regained. Upon engaging working memory, the patient may still be without physical power, unable to speak and in some cases unable to swallow: basically, behave like a baby - but you cannot and must not treat the patient as if they are a baby. The ABI survivor's inability to communicate what they are thinking is the true injury. Complex knowledge systems are still thought… they are just not expressed. Furthermore, in most cases, the grown, physical body may persist in child-like behavior commiserate with the survivor's subconscious, self-projected age. As the individual modulates through the recovery process, they will be reminded of social cues and mores, but this can be a grueling period of forgetfulness and self-discovery for any survivor.

The importance of allowing independence after reawakening to consciousness is vitally an integral component towards future, observable successes expected and realized post-rehabilitation. Otherwise, if you allow your own sadness to permeate the victim's personal awareness, you may contribute to bouts of persistent depression in the survivor or even something worse.

Never initiate in discussions where your survivor's life goals pre-injury are concerned. I understand how unbelievably lost you might feel lying in the hospital bed and coming to grips with the reality of the impacts attributed to brain trauma. For the parents, guardians, friends and other family members, it's super serious that you don't project ideologies of grief, loss, frustration or even hopelessness onto the minds of survivors. The nurses will likely be administering pain medicines, possibly a morphine drip and making sure the biological processes are functioning properly. One of the blessings for those having experienced TBI though, is that the survivor's emotions may very well be con-fuddled. As a result of temporal lobe injury, the innate lenience towards crying becomes disconnected and remains unavailable to the survivor for several years.

I'm unaware of the grief and fear encountered by loved ones inside the hospital waiting room or survivor's hospital room. The graciousness and restorative encouragement you can offer your survivor though, is the sweetest medicine anyone can afford. The after-life of survivors may become a conundrum of hidden meanings as previous life-goals, hopes and dreams appear to be... stolen. Be prepared to initiate growth in new talents perhaps unknown to the survivor, they need your positive, forward-leaning encouragement.

During the recovery process, there will come a moment when the survivor's workable memory triggers into function. As a family member, friend or court-appointed guardian - whomever plans to walk through the recovery process with the survivor - you must always be ready for the moment when the memory of the survivor's shadow-self reappears. Write out motivations you can share with your loved one before this happens.

The shadow-self is a concept that I'm introducing with this book because from my personal ethnography, I have found that some survivors don't readily have ideologies to express themselves when referring to that which they thought, before the traumatic event(s) unfolded. Verbosity plagues survivors of sTBI. While trying to get everything out that they're thinking at a given moment, this can lead to lengthy phrases and sometimes result in the survivor's forgetting of ideas or conversational points they were going to say. Conscious awareness of one's acquired difference(s) is a radically different concept than being injured. These nuggets of wisdom should not be orally shared during the preliminary phases of the recovery process, in my opinion, because part of understanding ourselves is learning these truths firsthand. Knowing that one is different from her/is shadow-self, residing in a hospital gown provides a paradigm of subconscious safety that means life will continue and healing may be fostered. At moments throughout the recovery process outside the hospital, though, the patient will take cognizance when self-assessing themselves. It's an extremely fine line here in realizing one's own perceived deficits and manifesting some sense of face, socially; while consistently dismissing thoughts of hopelessness and despair.

Always make allowances for child-like fascination in the self, regardless of physical age. Continue engaging on the age-level of the patient's physical body. Even though the patient may be unable to manifest adult-like behavior in their speech, they may likely still conceptualize thoughts respective to their age and education levels. Reasons for this are many, but can be summarized as how the brain can be affected. For most of humanity, names of people, places and ideas are stored near the blood brain barrier between the skull and dura matter; but the trained processes in thinking and actions are "hard-wired," as it could be said, deeper inside the central areas of the brain. Although they may not say it, people treating them as if they were toddlers will ultimately be grossly frustrating. The overall recovery process is going to take substantial time, effort, kindness, patience and calm than can be considered possibly imaginable, especially at the start.

I don't want my book to be a complete suppositional testament of some perceived experience, but I do want to share evidence of lying in the hospital. Let me say that my family-of-origin did a remarkable job of helping me recover; and I don't have any issues with my Dad. However, I have a faint memory of one day being hooked up to some machines and my Dad stooped down to give me a hug as I laid in bed. He said, "My son, oh, honey, I just love you so much, we've been praying for you this morning." The memory I have here is not necessarily concerning my Dad, but what I was thinking. He kind of rested on the bed and had his cheek next to mine. I just recall that he was crying, and I was lost. I still couldn't speak, but I was thinking, "Good grief, what's wrong with you?! Help, I can't breathe!" To the innocent, a thousand year stare may sound humorous, but I share this to let you know that speaking to the age of the physical body may be more appropriate than speaking to what the survivor can manifest.

Hope will guide you through recovery. Remain open to every outcome peacefully engaging with the injured and learn to separate your emotions through the discipline of journaling. Even though your existence will every once in awhile appear dejected to yourself and the patient, keep reminding yourself and others, it's the centered sanctity of calm that makes surviving successful.

"Out of the heart," he said, "come evil thoughts." Therefore the soul or principle of action is not in the brain according to Plato but in the heart according to Christ.

— Jerome
Matthew 15:19

CHAPTER 3

EMERGENCE

While highly trained professionals encourage your survivor's body achieve homeostasis, from the moment of trauma the survivor's brain works overtime to gain even one moment of rest. As most of us know, the brain consists of approximately 75% water. In addition to being one of the most watery organs of the human body, 60% of its mass is comprised of fat. If you or your survivor is among those of us with "closed-head sABIs," it's best to prepare for the worst while patients are still in the Intensive Care Unit (ICU). I am so very sorry that present circumstances have brought you to this book for guidance and discovery; but it's my intention to help you find a glimmer of hope, whatever your case may be.

Going forward, I implore you, the reader, to exhibit emotional boundaries with your survivor(s) from this moment on. Every traumatic experience that occurs is a terrible twist in consciousness; but today, there is more hope afforded to the plight of accepting sABIs. Humanity presently engages extra amounts of holism with regards to the brain's sensitivities more than ever before. In this chapter, I'm going to walk you through the structure of the brain. This should be of staunch interest to loved ones while sitting in the waiting room, but I can only imagine the kind of shock you're experiencing. If you are a survivor of severe TBI, I hope this exploration into the human brain can begin to help you continue healing emotionally. Highlights from my personal ethnography with recovery will come later in the book. At this moment though, I want to focus on helping you through these initial moments of unyielding questions.

Immediately following severe trauma, the ABI becomes a biological event of survival. Cranial bleeding, swelling, bone-cracking fissures, fractures and unraveling tissues and further damages are all possible problems encountered at the moment of impact. Emergency signals from the autonomic nervous system literally go haywire inside the body at this point, rendering the patient helpless. Perhaps important, when you're describing the severity of your loved one's injuries and pain, remember that the human brain, all three pounds of it, cannot actually feel pain since there are no pain receptors in the physical make-up of the brain itself. The brain can think of pain all over the body, but if the doctors have to introduce a shunt to relieve cranial fluid, the dura matter of the brain won't feel this.

The cerebricity responsible for our ability to manifest life subconsciously is in a single word, multifarious. An old wives' tale, and even some believing they were articulating "modern medicine," stated that human beings only used about 10% of their brain. The truth remains though, that every component has a unique function in regulating the homeostasis of the living corpse. The non-traumatized human brain in everyday life is said to produce enough electricity to power a light-bulb. To accomplish this feat, the average brain requires at least 20% of a person's blood supply, in addition to 20% of the total body's oxygen intake. I'm sure those numbers increase exponentially during times of shock or trauma.

As technology and research of the human condition continues, so does the concrete awareness of the working abilities of the brain. No matter how difficult the trauma, you must prepare for the reality that the brain may never fully amend to its pre-traumatic state. In other words, the survivor will very likely never be identical to the person you knew pre-trauma, even though many similarities persist. Each brain has within it the ability to uncover thousands of coping mechanisms by establishing new ways of functioning and bodily conditioning. In our present society, many believe a brain injury ought to be classified as short-term injuries. As humanity becomes increasingly aware, it's evident that sABIs are in fact classified as life-long handicaps because the injured brain is unable to return to it's non-traumatized state.

In some capacities, depending on where the brain experiences trauma, there will always be significant deficits, with some qualities especially prominent. In looking to supply a broad overview of severe brain injuries, it will help to become familiar with brain anatomy, structure and physiology. In short order, we can divide the overall head into five main groupings: 1) the skull and facial bones, 2) the nerves to the head and neck, 3) the blood vessels of the skull, 4) the brain, and 5) general trauma (D Derry Brown 1943). While being somewhat out-dated, this article from the Virginian Law Review walks us through the brain injury extremely well, and provides some otherwise lofty terminology that will likely be heard from the doctors while caring for a loved one.

Brown begins in discourse concerning that the human skull is just like any other bone in that if sufficient pressure or trauma is ensued, its "liable to fracture" or crack. The only difference in these bones is in the function they serve, each one vital to survival. But perhaps, for this book, we may speculate that the brain itself is the most extraordinary key to survival. This means that the skull, for all intents and purposes, serves protecting the organ-in-chief. In cases common to closed-head brain injuries, the skull will divide into solid, large pieces, which are termed comminuted fractures, because they don't involve tiny, splintered fragments. It's also possible that these comminuted fractures may radiate to the bowl on which the brain rests and cause a basal fracture, which ultimately disrupts air passages to the ear canal or nose, or even "channels through which pass nerves to the facial muscles" (D Derry Brown 1943).

You may remember from anatomy classes that there are a total of twenty-seven facial bones. Compared to most bones of the human anatomical structure, the facial bones are extremely delicate. Unlike bones surrounded by muscles, the facial bones are stationary at all times, with one exception being the mandible, which aids us in mastication… i.e. when we eat.

Nerves to the head and neck are important for body movement and the five senses. The five senses are made possible by the following nerves: the *olfactory* (smell); the *optic* (vision); the *trigeminal* (general sensation); *vagus nerves* (taste); and the *vestibulocochlear* nerve (hearing and balance). The facial nerves help in allowing humans to express their emotions physically, while the glossopharyngeal provides humans with the ability to express the emotions orally, communicate with others in their environment and taste foods using the back of the tongue. The oculumotor, trochlear, abducens, and hypoglossal nerves have more to do with overall body movement.

The brain is the master organ that monitors emotional feelings, physical well-being, and the tenant of motional freedom (Beats & Whitten 2010). While a common sense bestowed explanation as applied to the brain, it has taken millennia for humankind to uncover this truth. Across cultures and throughout time, there have been interesting views on the location of the seat of the personality of individuals. For one, the ancient Egyptians believed that the heart controlled the human body and thought. It could be that on the banks of the Nile, the priesthood described the teachings of the broken heart when speaking of a brain injury. When embalmers mummify the dead body, they spoon the dura material of the master organ through the nasal cavity and eventually discard it.

Fortunately, such a procedure is not practiced during the Common Era for the dead or the living. Nevertheless, the brain damage of a closed head injury can be extremely real and can manifest profound effects in the afterlife of said traumas. Ancient Egypt, that great kingdom of mystery in the ancient world, had fooled everyone for several hundred years. He also pointed out and maintained that the master organ, the heart, was the seat of governance of the human psyche. In the hieroglyphs their line of thinking follows: the brain doesn't move to keep blood flowing… it's the heart! When cadavers were used in Greece to study the human body and not glorify it through mummification, the Greek physician Alkamon (0400 BC) may have been the first to provide evidence that the brain and heart work together to make the body functional. There was no place though in said reasoning for the ideology of consciousness.

The brain can continue to function without oxygen for up to 6 minutes, so if oxygen is not provided after this point, the brain cells begin to die out. If the brain is deprived of oxygen for more than eight minutes, the person is likely to suffer permanent brain damage. You will remember from high school biology, that we humans are born with more brain cells than we will produce in the course of our lives. This is partly because the brain stops growing at age 18. Brain injury is not classified by the loss of presumptive brain cells, however, or even always by which area. But where oh where is the seat of consciousness? Preparation for an in-depth conversation regarding humanity's holistic understanding flows through a lens of comparative religion.

Determining the severity of a brain injury depends upon two pieces of information you may potentially overhear medical professionals discuss during your time in the waiting room or while reviewing patient records. Experts do not assess the severity of blood loss or the impact to the skull, whether the injury is opened or closed. They will use two pieces of information to arrive at a numerical measure of severity. The first is the initial score on the Glasgow Coma Scale, (see dictionary). Such is a descending, numerical score that starts at 15. The second number, which is the most important number, is the actual summary score given in lost times.

So described Loss of Consciousness is a strange thought to me. I'd like to share some perhaps fascinating, qualitative insight into what happens as a survivor in a coma or vegetative state. I will tell you that in this section I am not going to repeat the countless stories of people who were unconscious. In part, I find this notion misleading, because anyone who first wakes up inside a hospital setting will undoubtedly open their eyes to bright light. Not meant to be offensive to anyone, I understand that some people hold that idea quite firmly... it certainly hasn't been my own experience. So everyone can rest assured: I have no working memory of that time.

There is an old Egyptian proverb that draws a round shape like the seasons, understanding is not taught, time develops in degrees. The wisdom of knowledge is the goalmouth allowing measurements for the whole circle. When the postulant is awake {lest someone claim the Crown appears to reveal that "it is but only the supplicant who's suddenly woken up"} and become unconscious {and patient}, for such is just the first degree.

As it is written, learning to put past the barrier of awareness fulfills the teachings of the nineteenth degree. Today, it seems that most have either forgotten or simply followed false teachings. Many of my fellow Americans stop growing up whenever they glorify their own logic in marking the six directions. According to my personal trajectory, I have discovered this: knowledge about such erudition has yet to be properly arranged.

They also say beside the Nile river, all organs work together as a general feature. Therefore, I have taken a small lot of the knowledge burden upon myself to present a smorgasbord of human knowledges about the mind-body continuum. When I was finishing my first book, Peribology: A Budding of Secrets (Facebook®), I had the idea to research several ideas about the seat of consciousness while in a comatose. For how shall we truly believe that the spirit is separate from the mind, if there shall remain in us no sense and memory of the heart which our forebears taught concerning this relationship? Or shall we be reformed toward the continuum only materially, but not fully in our consciousness? Do not fear the library.

> Peribology is open to all for use in deciphering myth and fact. However, at this time I must make mention of the current debacle creating restlessness between three of the major world religions. First of all, in the opinion of Peribology, those following Christian ideals should use more caution at being sensitive to the truth that there is no god, but God and he is one. Going to the first writings of the books of Moses, the delivering agent who had seen and witnessed through hearing Yahweh's character — something Muslims, Christians, and Jews all believe I might add — we find a nugget of reality within the creation story of the Genesis. The Torah tells us that God said, "Let us make humankind in our image." To whom was God recorded as speaking? He wasn't; and its in that omission that anyone following Abraham's example is continually caught. In the same way that you can get to know a person on many different levels, I believe God's character is made manifest in the same manner. In the beginning, humans conceptualized themselves as man and woman. For some Jews, since there is no "afterlife," we are just bodies. As thinking increased, we at some point decided that we had souls which would continue to live on after our bodies died; perhaps after the first death of a human, when breath leaves the body. Some Muslims believe that the human being is a dichotomous union of soul and body. Then some Christians identified the human condition in threes: a mind, body, and spirit. Each unifying layer though has followed science as it helped us to understand our bodily processes. Most recently, the dynamisms continuum

has been divided into fours: mind, body, emotions and spirit (Sisson 2013).

Wait a minute, wait a minute! What if I do not see the heaven of religion? Are there just three component boxes for discussing human character? For many following their American teachings, atheism modulated the best dynamic example of mystery, thus being written in the heavens of education as the most powerful representative of science around the world. They will tell you that the presence or unpredictability as such an important force lies solely in the conceptual process of understanding creationism. It can seem surprising if you are a scientist to explain the brainchild and develop such boring knowledge of any need of God. In the culmination round, much of these responsibilities helped to strengthen the position of the atheist as they became certain of the unseen and henceforth, "God is no longer needed as a concept in such terms."

In addition, the postulant's pseudoscience described a secondary mechanism of action, such as what she/he might call panpsychism. Perhaps the belief that everything like quarks and atoms has consciousness actually suggests that drudgery is inherent in all elements and all reality. In other words, they say that in order for consciousness to develop, the machine or automatic input to the brain must have a spirit. However, even among their own issues are limitations or side effects when, for example, it comes to the natural explaining of how subjective consciousness arises in biological systems. That is, dualists believe that work has mechanical properties, but these changes have an external agency, separate from the mechanical.

Unless some wisdom regarding the catholic nonentity is active in cruel materialisms, the monitoring will of consciousness as associated with the primordial force of nature is also important. According to the original offerings and practical dictionary, the homunculus is thought to stir truth and create consciousness by communicating through cells, neurons, synapses, and synaposematic features in the brain. Hence, if the brain created consciousness individually, can it be said that the human brain cannot now be fully known unless universal thought first existed in the primitives? In other words, could it be that the first fruits fell from the Tree of Life because the war of heaven caused the big bang…? An open heart allows discussion, but let us leave all esoteric messages with others who have more understanding. After allowing everyone to gather, the ancient peoples' library of the divine could clarify such contemporary concerns with contemplation of the mind-body continuum.

Even in ancient times, students were influenced by their immediate teachers. Aristotle was tutored by Plato who was instructed by Socrates. Plato seems to have believed that a soul is independent of the body. It's the real me clothed in my body, which is not me. It may or may not have existed from the beginning of time, but it will survive for all eternity with the same personality it creates when joined to this body.

In his work entitled, *The Apology*, Plato provides his readers with a description of his teacher as he theorized about the concept of death just prior to dying. Socrates believed that there were only a total of two plausible outcomes involving human death: "either there would be *nothingness* after death," or, "as some believe, we experience a change as the soul migrates from here to another place." Plato seems to have believed the latter because he also said that human beings "must bear in mind this one truth: no evil befalls the good person; neither in life or after, [because] God does not neglect the individual." However there is no certainty that Plato accepted the secondary possibility because, as Plato wrote in his *Republic* it is necessary to teach the masses ideas that are false, or ideas he termed, "essential truths," in order to control them from acting "improperly".

As per yet another prolific writing, *De Anima* (On the Soul), Aristotle rejects Plato's notion that the soul is independent. He contended that the soul is the life force that makes it possible for something to live and think. It is "the *cause* or *source* of the living body," as well as "the essential '*what-ness*' of the body." By deduction, that which comprises the soul [must be made of] several items. In humans, the soul is comprised of five parts or systems: the nutritive system, the appetitive (desires and passions), senses, locomotion, and thinking. Since they are alive, plants and animals must also have souls, but not all five parts. Plants, according to Aristotle, only have the nutritive part of the soul. Animals have four of the five pieces, but lack the component which fosters thinking and reason.

Aristotle stated that the "mind" could never be destroyed and that which makes up individual "intellect," will continue to exist after the death of the body. Old people have difficulty thinking not because the mind has deteriorated, but because the vehicle, the body, holding the mind has deteriorated. This is similar to what happens when a person is drunk or sickly; the vessel of the Brain, i.e. the human body refuses to allow the mind work. However, as he reasoned, even though the mind lives on, that same surviving intellect knows nothing regarding its prior existence.

Conversely, the Taoism offers an interesting take on the mind-body continuum. Perhaps the oldest tradition of human knowledge emanated from ancient China. For example, they believe humans are derived of three huny, "souls", and seven p'o, "spirits". As a matter of theory, there is little difference between an idea of three souls and another of one soul and spirit. It is stated that the hun corresponds to yang, or male principle, and at death it ascends to heaven. On the other hand, the p'o corresponds to the yin, or female principle, and at death remains on earth.

As to the three huny after death, one ascends, one remains, and the third is tied to the fate of the corpse. Again it is said that one represents the vegetative, one the animal, and the third the moral principle. In this lens, the first and second huny follow cessation like the body, but the third, which contains character is immortal. The seven spirits are the five senses and two functioning actions of the limbs. With regards to near-death-experiences, however, Taoists believe the mind (Shen) is not with the body, i.e. Po, during coma.

When assessing comatose through this Chinese philosophical lens, the question of the spirit bearing mindfulness has been given not answerable. The functionality of the brain however has not died because the Hun, which is the soul, is clinging unto the body. Finding out what to expect inside such biological housekeeping and stasis, it is the heart (and not the spirits) taking control over the body during Loss of Consciousness. Furthermore, it is said that the individual will continue to live as long as the soul remains in control of the body, because the physical body cannot be released to the Earth until the mind (despite the fact of its nonfunctionality) allows the soul to leave.

Western understanding of the mind-body continuum is similar. Many Western, religious believers have faith in a spiritual judgement between a heaven and hell. There seems built upon Eastern traditions similarities in the mind-body continuum, because the spirit or soul governs an individual's functionality as to when the body may be given back to the earth.

For a competent context of comatose, consider such a new construct of the continuum. If we look to the paradigm of some, that we are made in the image of God, or evolved to that state, why is it so hard for so many of us to believe that each person is not also designed to be 3-in-1? Although, I tend to find wisdom in the Eastern traditions, my Western translation of their philosophy might involve the Central Nervous System (CNS), the Autonomic Nervous System (ANS), and the body. We know that especially during comatose, the CNS does not respond, i.e. the mind is asleep, while the recesses of the brain operate within the ANS and help regulate bodily functions. The ANS won't let the body die, it governs the body. So we might've said that the ANS could be the spirit or soul of a person, the CNS as the mind, while certainly, the physical person is the body.

In 2009, the public theology organization of *Theos* conducted a research study in the United Kingdom of people's belief in life after death. Of the random 2,060 UK citizens interviewed, 53% stated belief in life after death, whereas only 70% of those surveyed believed in the concept of the human body having a soul. They uncovered several interesting findings that give us an idea about beliefs in Western thought. The article went on to say that 2 out of every 5 people in the UK believe in some phenomena of "ghosts". A total of 15% UK citizens interviewed confirmed they had personally experienced some form of 'flying spirits'. The UK survey did not differentiate between soul or spirit, and whether or not people believe either or both of these exist within some conscious mind-body continuum (*telegraph.uk* April 13, 2009).

Conversely, in the US, FOX news administered a Gallop Poll Survey in 2004 finding that an overwhelming 92% of US Americans believe in any proof concept of God. Still, such a critical concept is loosely construed from a broad perspective, because of the total interviewed, only 3/4 believe in a hell, while 85% believe in a heaven. Interestingly, the group of interviewees, all between the ages of 18-34, showed a striking 34% believe in any concept of ghost-like activity while a different group of 34% shared belief in UFOs. Who can really say what happens to our internal energy when we go under for surgery or are unconscious for long periods of time?

Some may remember this horror film, "The Fourth Kind." The movie tells the true-to-life story of a researcher and his family after he dies mysteriously. I do not want to highlight anything else from this movie except for the fact that in Nome, Alaska; several individuals experience a type of out-of-body experience while they sleep, or are unconscious. I find it strange that researchers never looked to the original stories of how Nome was founded, and if any community perceptions might stem from the original population of the area's Native inhabitants. I also find it interesting to contrast this modern story to other cultures that developed clearly defined ideas concerning the mind-body continuum.

The ancient Egyptians distinguished between ba, the soul of consciousness; ka, the dream-body; and khu, the spirit or intelligence. During life the ba together with other spiritual factors was believed to inhabit the ab (heart) or perishable body. Fundamentally, the Egyptian religion taught that for the sake of the ba's welfare, the body ought be preserved. Therefore, a host of methods were used to preserve or mummify the dead bodies of great individuals. Once the perishable body was wrapped, the mummy became an idea all it's own, known as sahu. Following finite rituals, the Ancient Egyptians stored vast amounts of wealth to help their mummies succeed in the afterlife as they resided in their dark abodes or tombs, pa t'etta, i. e., houses great-everlasting.

> Here we see the word "brain" occurring for the first time in human speech, as far as it is known to us; and in discussing injuries affecting the brain, we note the surgeon's effort to delimit his terms as he selects for specialization a series of common and current words to designate three degrees of injury to the skull indicated in modern surgery by the terms "fracture", "compound fracture," and "compound comminuted fracture," all of which, the ancient commentator carefully explains (Breasted 1920).

The seat of consciousness and intelligence was from the earliest times regarded by the Egyptians as both the heart and the bowels or abdomen. Our surgeon, however, has observed the fact that injuries to the brain affect other parts of the body, especially in his experience, the lower limbs. He notes the drag or shuffle of one foot, presumably the partial paralysis resulting from a cranial wound, and the ancient commentator carefully explains the meaning of the [now] obsolete word used for, "shuffle" (Breasted 1920).

Many Westerners have been trained to speak of human beings' bodies, souls and spirits. My opinion tends to lead us back to Chinese medical theory where we conceptualize that the soul governs the body's responses to the mind. In other words, as long as the body is functioning, the mind controls the soul. Some NAI cultures believe that while the body is sleeping, the mind is powerful enough to allow the soul wander throughout the earth. When a person is murdered in their sleep, this is what causes ghosts because the mind and soul never rejoined before the body stopped functioning (Estes 2006).

Additionally, we could even go so far as to discuss the nervous systems as the basis of an individual's personality. The sympathetic nervous system could be seen as a person's spirit; while the para-sympathetic nervous system could be described the person's vessel (body). The enteric nervous system might triggered by the soul or conscious character of an individual, which would direct us to an African tribal belief in which the stomach is the soul. However, such a classification needs to be investigated by the academic community.

Beliefs in Shamanism portray a clear foundation to where the mind is able to leave the body during any unconscious activity, including sleep, illness, and especially during dreams (among folklore this could be esteemed as astral projection; but folk anthropology is for some other writer). Even still, there is evidence from a religiously fundamentalist perspective to where the soul is comforted by the Name some call, Jesus, and restorative peace is provided the ailing patient. In 2011, a 4 year-old male, who had gone in for a surprise surgery, told newscasters that he had been comforted by Jesus and had seen long lost relatives in their early twenties. He vividly portrayed playing ball in a natural field of green grass with his grand-parents.

As for academia, the mind-body continuum is approached from an ideological standing in consciousness. According to a researcher of the early 20th century, one's own character as a viable reality exists only because of one's awareness. She further explains the following, including the following without limitation. 1) The reality of oneself is basal to experience in as much as perception is required. 2) The nature of oneself ascribes a peripheral motive inverted within any body's persistence. 3) The depths of character are only as complex as oneself may be considered unique. 4) The interplay of the previous qualities result in one's personality being made manifest through a communicative output via their spirit (Caulkins 1908).

In my opinion, the first three descriptors explain that which in the human being is natural. Personality, individual choice, reactions, opinions and attitudes are the express result of the body's soul. Therefore, classifying modern medical knowledge through an old world lens can be taxing. So regardless of what your beliefs concerning the mind-body continuum, scientists of human behaviors know that the most vital healing and rest happen externally, along the periphery right before humans wake up. Internally however, the body restores itself during deepest sleep when we are first asleep and as we lie unconscious during phases of REM sleeping.

A full belly makes a dull mind.

– Benjamin Franklin

CHAPTER 4

CONSCIOUSNESS REKINDLED

Now that we've reached the next phase in the recovery process, remember the brain is not a bone. Following the wake up, be prepared for the fact that it will never be exactly like our neighborhood Dr. Media Pump-Fake portrays. Just because an individual awakens from unconscious slumber, patients are not automatically guaranteed "smooth sailing" through recovery, as when its an isolated bone like the femur or humorous. Let us remember that the cause of comatose extends quite far from some simplified ideology of stolen consciousness that is the closed-head brain injury.

For survivors, "finding oneself," is not easily restored by reminders of behavior patterns and "the way things were". Survivors cannot just upload data from a hard-drive back-up. In the veracity of waking up and realizing what's happened, the mind will have difficulty remembering what came before. It seems like a divergent exchange of reason for child-like clichés, but it's the new way of thinking with which your survivor may be infused.

In addition, a significant trademark of TBI will be realized by its hiddenness. There will be moments inside the next 10-15 years where you will see the survivor exhibiting behaviors exactly like the person you knew pre-trauma. However, if you manipulate those characteristics to persist, you will undoubtedly exhaust the survivor. It takes an unnatural amount of energy to override the tendency to be different. You may hear them express this as saying, "It's so hard to be myself."

Awareness to one's new personality type will take time. If, as a caretaker or parent, you highlight these differences to others, you may actually create distance between yourself and the survivor. They may think subconsciously, "I'm trying so hard to be as you knew me before the injury, but I don't know how!" Words may not be attainable to the survivor at the moment of inquiry, but later on, in a few years, these concepts can ring true.

Every memorable moment is recorded by the human brain from 6-months to the present day of a person's lifetime. In the moment of trauma, losing one's consciousness erases the working memories of every action, thought, moral, acceptable behavior and learned social knowledge. Imagine, if you will, that each memory is written down on identical sheets of paper and filed away for safe keeping in the brain's office. Some might do this next task more easily than others; but remember the opening theme song of the Mary Tyler Moore Show? Almost like the idea of a Grecian sprite, the Mary Tyler Moore inside the brain has every memory in her hand and stores them in her beret during the theme song. At the close of the song, she hikes it to the sky, singing, "We're gonna make it after all!" Like paper money thrown from the top of an apartment building, every memory, association and some skills twitter and flit through the air until finally landing on a busy road.

In such a way, every connection in the brain is scattered and wiped clean along the periphery, making it fundamentally impossible to produce seasonable connections commiserate with working memory for quite a bit of time after the traumatic experience. Over the next ten years, at least, the survivor's job is to accumulate all these knowledges (papers) and file them away, correctly, while operating through recovery and life as though these memories are in a clean office of the brain. It gets better after years of recovery, but for the sake of your survivor, make allowances for years of recovery and don't move too fast.

Depending on where the skull fractures struck the dura matter of the brain, your survivor may not know who you are, or in rare circumstances, even of whom they are themselves. This is what the professional world will classify as "amnesia." At the same time, if your survivor remembers people but not events, this is called, "retrograde amnesia."

When addressing memory of survivors post-reintegration, it's proper to remember that there are three different types: executive [working], explicit and implicit memories. Explicit memory is the conscious, intentional recollection of previous experience and information. Implicit memory on the other hand is a type of memory in which previous experience aids in the performance of behaviors or tasks without consciously recalling any previous experience. Interesting to note that life post-ABI is devoid of explicit memory, especially during the initial weeks of recovery.

General memory can be further phrased into two main categories. The first is declarative, which is either episodic or semantic. Episodic memory is the memory of autobiographical events (explicit memory covering times, places, and associated emotions; i.e. contextual knowledge). Semantic memory on the other hand, refers to the memory of facts and experiences (explicit memory covering meanings and understandings gained through life experience; i.e. concept-based knowledge).

Procedural memory is the second division of general memory including procedural knowledges, which help us perform skills and simple classical conditioning, among others. For severe head injury, procedural (implicit) memory will seem to have vanished, but re-learning of simple tasks like standing, walking, swallowing, writing, etc will happen fast for some patients but slower for others. I was able to walk, swallow, and even communicate before I had completely regained consciousness.

In order to teach survivors in the hospital setting, professionals use a variety of theories to present their educational strategies. One method of instruction in cognitive therapy allows for something they call behaviorism theory. In behaviorism, age-appropriate learning results when patients begin to alter their observable behaviors in order to present themselves at a certain age-level.

Next, trained professionals will take into account the amount of time spent in post-traumatic amnesia and afterward they will score or grade the survivor according to the Rancho Los Amigos Scale of Cognitive Functioning (1-10), which changes at different speeds after the first scoring per individual, much like my age-equivalence spectrum, which inherently is meant to engage the survivor in the decision-making rationale of their individual treatment.

"To know where one is going, each must first know where they've been."

— Bryan Sisson *in* Peribology

CHAPTER 5

CLAIMING THE AFTERLIFE

I doubt William Edward Hickson gave a second thought when he published that unnerving little poem. I could tell you to try until you can try no more, but that seems a bit extreme. The afterlife for every survivor is riddled with a kind of hit-or-miss accuracy almost like a kind of athletic dropsy, and an inability to keep up with standard operations. No matter what you decide to do with yourself after the traumatic event… don't ever allow yourself to give up! If at first you don't succeed, remain on the course, become doughty and try again.

I myself would be remiss if I ever conveyed that I never wanted to give up during recovery, but you and your survivor(s) may naturally feel so consumed by the acquired burdens of TBI that you might wish to do just that. On the one hand, it's not intelligible to compare traumatic experiences. Although, on the other hand, it's an ideological mandate for you and your survivor(s) to maintain that someone, somewhere has experienced way worse. Since ideas of struggle and pain are subjective, it's also befitting of everyone to remember the following sentiment.

If human beings had no rational sociobiology, we all would be uniquely affected by handicaps of all types. Humanity has become endowed with operational knowledge of our world, overall. But none of us could ever have rationalized a perceived need of wisdom until we were old enough to possibly have burnt our fingers on a hot stove. Fundamentally, people learn that if something causes pain, it's bad! Therefore, I won't do that again. From the moment we manifest working memory in our first lives, we continue to grow, learn and mature.

By the time we're about through 12 years of primary school, we've learned and likely produced empathetic behaviors in conjunction with a hierarchical social structure in the school culture right alongside the appropriate behaviors permitted or disallowed in our individual home cultures. Such intricate displays of perplexing intelligences - good, bad; us, other - continues with us into our adult lives. As covered in chapter 1, handicaps and disabilities - physical differences, acquired or pre-existing - were just one more addition to the complexity of judging ourselves immaturely.

"She climbs a tree and scrapes her knee; her dress has got a tear..." is an opening chorus line concerning Mariá in Roger and Hammerstein's, *Sound of Music*. It's natural for humans to judge one another. Can it be rude? Sometimes. Hurtful? Yes. Feeble-minded? Assuredly. Understanding humanity when we are young is normally sheltered and innocently sincere.

If Liberty Six-Pack has a cold and sneezes nearby, students learn to excuse themselves and wash their hands; so as to decrease the likelihood of bacterial or viral infection. Most peers in our biology classes conceived that washing hands often was generally a good idea. In health classes we further learned of the differences between bacterial infections, diseases and viruses. Janey Long-Legs pinkey-swore with her best friends that she would never hang out with people having weird bumps on their faces.

Furthermore, we observed throughout the semester, learning what things could be transmitted and what illnesses could be treated. Broken bones heal fast enough, flu and common cold might take you out for a week, but pneumonia, smallpox or the kissing disease could make one miss school for longer periods of time. We even learned that some people sick from viruses come into the massage clinic.

I could have reacted to these at-the-time hurtful premonitions, but its best to leave the past in the past. In several ways, the USA has made great strides in procuring equality for all people when comparing human rights to other nations. But, we're still not there yet! Its as though the behaviors of humanity must always hold someone or something as less than they. Its my opinion here, but I think society should undergo some kind of education en mass that will explain how ABIs and TBIs *cannot* be caught, spread or encouraged.

Such truths may be difficult for families that focus on the family's position inside their community. Flippant and knee-jerk reactions often encourage silent assumptions of others. I have a dear friend who often drives her car when we go out to eat downtown. I ride along so we can be environmentally sensitive. We had taken a wrong exit one time when we were headed to the House of Blues. And what a surprising exit it was! There was an gentleman standing on the corner rather disheveled and holding a sign that read, "Got fired: HUNGRY." As we approached the red light, I heard a thundering, Lock! The gentleman looked at her car and rolled his eyes. He then sat down in his lawn-chair and threw his sign in the tall grass. While I don't know that he had a brain injury, his reactions left me thinking of what would have been my response.

It can take at most, anywhere from ten to fifteen or even twenty years for survivors to distance themselves from the on-set of brain injury and successfully match their mind to body. As we discussed earlier, the different types of memory available to the normal adult who has not experienced trauma, has an agility, almost second nature, to fit past experiences, i.e. explicit memory, into any number of scenarios based on contextual conversation. Many fellow TBI impacted individuals I've met within support-groups, tell stories of how their memories flooded because of a reaction seen, a scent smelled, a touch felt, etc.

I propose that for we survivors, the act of calling upon explicit memories becomes mirrored in a way so that instead of living with explicit memory, our brains project explicit memories onto a screen of the mind to where we always watch, but rarely feel, as many of us become unable to express casual conservation in tandem with sociocultural cues. For example, when a group of friends might be talking about their mothers and comparing childhood stories of getting in trouble, I would most likely stay seated quietly unable to grasp a vivid memory to share from my own life. But put me in the same setting with wafting aromas of bacon and pancakes, and I quickly recall a time when Mom swatted my behind for taking bacon from the plate before the family had been seated for breakfast.

Smells are often the avenue of channeling explicit memories for myself, but I know of countless others who will say that it is touch that produces the same effect. Its important to remember that because of where the impact injures your survivor, incurred brain injuries are like fingerprints: not one identical to another. The commonalities in brain injuries do not come from the type of trauma induced, nor are they proven similar by individual lengths of time in comatose. In recovery though, when the brains are attempting to reconstruct and rewire, professionals find the identical traits that make brain injuries so frustratingly alike.

Regardless of the type of trauma causing a closed-head brain injury, all closed-head TBIs experience memory lapse. Even though similarities persist, there is no certainty that says a brain injury or even concussion, for that matter, will end up in a specific state of healing. The memory lapse is due to the shearing introduced through sudden inertia. When I lay in the hospital in 1999, hooked up to life support as my parents-of-origin identified my damaged body, that was the verbiage used to console my Mom and Dad. It was not until 2009, however, that I would be fully embodied with my own personal ethnography to explain that sentence, or this ideology of life overwhelmed by 'acquired brain trauma.'

Depending on the severity of 1) trauma, 2) comatose, and 3) recovery; the 'afterlife' will be proportionate to the brain's abilities for rewiring itself. During this time on what I refer to as the TABIÆS, the nervous system re-formed the mind-body continuum towards the return to homeostasis. The survivor's perceived homeostasis, though, may be plagued with a complex quandary of personal views towards the idea of disability. Decisions of disability levels are to be termed by the individual and no one else, unless a trained professional.

When we are about the age of junior high or high school, and many times earlier, we learn that telling children of the friends we visit, "You can't do this or that," is wildly inappropriate. Its their house for one, and its their children for another. What happens though when the situational roles are reversed during recovery? Some individuals outside your familial structure will complain that as one in recovery, you should be trying harder or doing better. Its a good idea to reflect on religious wisdoms to foster unending patience.

When the Buddha was alive in Asia, he said, "Each human becomes the author of their individual health or disease." Many will be rude about your survivorship after acquiring life-changing injury, but know this truth. Be thankful for them, because without their unique opinions, humanity would be overrun by despair.

Freedom-of-speech is a double-edged sword. You either have to accept that human beings will on occasion make mistakes, or you have to never allow people to speak their mind. I am not condoning hurtful dialogue or behaviors, but I know that if we have any hope of procuring this inspiring democracy, every one has to constantly be the bigger person. Religious teachers are not inspiring because they have some unattainable methodology of creating unique perceptions to life. They inspire us because they motivate us to be more noble than we present ourselves to be. With encouragement, survivors of all types are made to take the high road in my opinion.

What would the United States of America look like if all of us took the high road? Media outlets would not be able to encourage or dissuade opinions because we understand that human beings make mistakes. Arguing would be over - dysfunctional Congressional bodies would be of the past - and we would co-exist in a manner of servitude and love for one another. Is this a reality? Certainly not! Could it be?

Humans tailor their awareness of world events by obtaining information only from outlets that "politically" espouse the same views as themselves. Arguments persist, our national legislative bodies are sadly out of sync with one another, and the majority of humans base their amount of willingness to live with a neighbor of differing views on whether or not they believe in the correct deity!

Moreover! In the midst of this malevolent melee, there is an unseen, allowable tendency to exuberantly identify and proclaim physical differences in public and in private throughout the USA. In some cases, survivors are bereft of any hospitable culture all over the world. I am not saying that due to acquired differences, your personality will automatically extend patience to others who objectify you as limited. I am sharing with you that if the high road is traveled more frequently, the journey will be additionally tolerable.

A friend of mine from Nebraska served in the first wave of soldiers in Iraq in 2003. After experiencing a blunt trauma-closed head injury, he was unconscious for 7 days and 18 hours. Jason looks totally well, but his ability to fight hadn't rewired yet when he came home. Nearly 35 years old, he was confused about why he was in the Middle East for several days. He was sent home to recover, and is continually improving with his acquired differences.

Even though he did not have the kind of recovery like I was so blessed to experience, would any of you talk down to him and say that he needs to go back to work serving our country at the recovery phase he ended up at?! I hope you wouldn't do such a thing. His cousins were concerned when he asked to see his mother, who he picked out as they wheeled him into the American Airlines Suite at DFW. Mrs. Robinson exclaimed, "Its like the first time you got home from boy-scouts!" and she proceeded to hug him in his wheelchair, while the entire group of well-wishers that gathered to welcome him home looked at each other, quietly.

Indeed, to the outsider, it seems quite supercilious that an older woman would speak of such a young situation to a 35 year-old soldier. Even so, how different the reactions by others would have been if they, too, had heard Jason speak of waking up in the veteran hospital and feeling like he was actually waking up after breaking his leg at boy-scouts some 20 years ago. She was merely reassuring him that she loved him just as he was, that day, that moment in time.

The reacquisition of real-time consciousness in many instances is not going to be performed quickly or attained instantaneously. We do not live our lives on the big screen. Not wanting to add insult to injury, people have got to conceptualize the reality of survivor's waking from comatose. Its not a soap opera. It will take an unbelievable amount of time to feel as though your survivor is "back".

With my personal ethnography, I've re-experienced thousands of "firsts," first time to chew, swallow, walk, speak... and the list goes on. But because of where my brain was hit, I never forgot complicated mathematics, how to read, or even how to play the piano. For example, while I didn't remember how to swallow, before memory was triggered, I sat on the bench at a piano and played, *Savior, Like a Shepherd Lead Us*. Those knowledges, the ones we learn during our formative years are maintained inside the interior storage sites of the brain, whereas people's names and social etiquette are closer to the periphery or outer edges of the brain, and whereby injured or lost until the brain finishes re-mapping.

One profoundly important concept is to remember not to speak of a TBI as if it were something to just heal, get over, and be done with. Traumatic experience with the brain is not just recovery-time changing; but often derives life-change, requiring presence on an ideological battle-ground where the survivor must learn new coping strategies, re-define the order of simple tasks, and consistently identifying the redefined steps put in place to eradicate those moments of forgetfulness, loneliness and confusion.

If you generate resolve to find mistakes in your survivor, you're going to find them, of that there is no contest. The severity and reoccurrence of a survivor's ability to make honest mistakes is a key factor in determining relationship validity. No matter what happens with the survivor's income, social status, education, health, or life, never make them feel inferior. My own family cannot read this and observe that mistakes were made in their treatment of me. At this point of my book, some say the analysis implements a false sense of lucidity, which often transpires during moments of grief and/or shock. Besides, I'm no perfect saint.

Where on earth does our ability to accommodate those living with a visible handicap come from?! Its a paradigm shift that I beseech humans to make. Obviously we have to be careful that we do not allow those fit to generate livelihood creep into a place that we would have to serve them or forgive them for being lazy! I get that! But what happens when doctors, psychologists, and the like determine an innocent, well-to-look adult does have serious brain injury, disability, and severe handicap? Is it true that we would just decide to mistreat that person because they go against our own frame of reference?! That the US Government would actually warrant the issue of BP license plates to an individual NOT showing one of the visible signs of disability? Could it be there are things going on in our world that we actually have to admit we know nothing about? "Wake up, O sleeper! Get away from the dead!"

In my own life, others projecting impatience onto me and looking away is the most hurtful, when I have no ability to explain my personal case because the words are simply not readily available. One of my biggest pet peeves is when I stop to think of a word, and the person with whom I'm conversing takes that moment to busy themselves with something else. I've never actually confessed this to anyone, but I think that's kind of rude.

If I am pressured to debate and argue, my mind literally freaks out; a fact that I know others encounter in this world. Through occupational therapy, and learning of ideological concepts at school, I have furthered my ability to argue, etc. but where the impact of TBI has encouraged such hardship, I have never fully been able to explain exactly what I mean at a moment's notice since pre-trauma. Not because I can't talk or because I'm unable to think of complete sentences, but because my TBI-impacted explicit memory almost forbids the task.

I see myself trying to explain these ideas in the past to less than intelligent people and being scoffed down because of a speech error or people just being rude about my facial features. Boundaries have freed me from needing to explain my case in every situation. And I encourage you to share Cloud & Townsend's, *Boundaries*, with your survivor. Because I know that I am right with my God, I am true to my own self. "What does that mean," you ask? It means that no matter what anybody wants to say about me, I have a brain injury.

If people want to say, "You haven't forgiven the folks at Ozark Christian College because you won't accept your injury as your uniquely 'created', new normal!" To which I would pose, "How can a bird fly if it has a broken wing?" I must share with you that these opening lines of conversation actually took place a few years ago on Facebook® with an old colleague that I haven't spoken to in some time.

One of the oldest traditions teaches that little baby Jesus was conceived in the womb of a Galilean virgin, Mary. Today, December 25, 2010, I am surprised by the religious. I am not Catholic, and have no qualms concerning the position of this paragraph. Interestingly however, some Catholics believe that since Mary birthed holiness, and since she is esteemed as female Saint to the "Universal" Papacy, a cherished belief about her being touched by the Divinity includes her freedom from pain.

I believe there was a birthing transpired; and I believe that Mary was a devout Jewess; but I will never believe that just because some "miracle" happened, there were also supernatural forces exercised so she might never experience physical pains of childbirth or physical pains during her lifetime. Moreover, just because a survivor of severe injury can look and act like they do not experience life-long disability, that does not translate they live a life free of bodily pains!

I am mortified to this day at the squawks and gossiping surrounding my person whenever someone thinks that I should not be treated as if I'm disabled. Nothing makes me more irate, and I do not mean to draw attention away from the purpose of this book, except to tell you that if you choose to keep your loved one on life-support, do not ever cast them aside in a moment of argument or some kind of questioning disbelief about the "miracle" that may have taken place for your survivor.

If you're really going to say that "we prayed for you, that you would be healed," and "you're not believing enough in the miracle, thats why you have pain;" you better very well be able to stomach your own judgement on that day, because I cannot, for the life of me, understand why parents, family members, friends and even acquaintances would so ardently take care of someone, love them, nurture them, and eventually say, "We will tolerate your presence no longer, because of the brain injury." This is one of the most serious points of this book. And I don't say this for me, I say this for the traumatized victims, if you're going to pay for life-support, family care, and countless therapies, I do not want you to ever tell your brain traumatized individuals down the road, "The recovery isn't working for us anymore and we just cannot bare the sight of you any longer, because we know what's best." You might as well pull the plug now, because everything you say from the moment they wake up will be judged by someone higher. If loving family boundaries are a-wash, it will make life miserably confusing post-trauma.

Beware of the Pandora box which is the process of TBI recovery. You may not like what is happening or what choices will be made in the end, but it is always your responsibility to the patient who recovers, no matter what happens.

Thankfully, there are holistic remedies that you can utilize to bring about emotional well-being and even restore happiness with yourself and/or your survivor. Your loved one, or good friend that has experienced brain trauma will appear difficult to figure out. You might think they're immature for their age, or even annoying in a way that never was before.

The hard part of rationalizing behaviors and emotions is entirely quite simple. Whenever I have social problems or am severely irritated with myself, a good friend who is also my chiropractor says, "Well, its just the brain injury; what can you do?" The answer is always inferred… nothing. After trying to figure out the problem for a few days, I am always surprised that his simple assessment is consistently accurate.

Herbs and Emotional Benefits

Lemon balm	sharpens wit
Catnip	relieves stress
Pinks	relieves melancholy

Borage	sustains courage
Sage	brings wisdom
Mint	provides refreshment
Sweetbriar	spreads cheer
Basil	highlights your good qualities

The smells of these herbs are good for restoring peace of mind when the patient is tired or restless. While my Great-Grandmother might say, "Cleanliness is next to godliness;" survivors do operate best in clean, fresh environments. Its easier for the brain to operate in a clean atmosphere than it is when the setting is cluttered like the brain. Aromatherapy is a useful non-invasive trick, and the above list, gives a few suggestions that might help you or your survivor on the road to recovery. A multi-vitamin is usually beneficial, but you should always consult your local pharmacist for questions pertaining to herbal remedies.

Regardless of strategies used in your past, especially when your survivor may have been younger, its important to remember that the brain injury subtly changes everything. Personality traits, favorite tastes, and even favorite smells. It may be, for sake of argument, that as the brain is rewiring itself it uncovers new sensations that permeate present consciousness. I remember when I was in the hospital, my favorite juice was Welch's® Cranberry-Grape juice, something I absolutely detested pre-trauma. In addition, my favorite smell changed from freshly-baked bread to bacon and breakfast fiddles. These can be explained away of course as matters of environmental conditioning through my second birth: the moment I regained consciousness.

Despite the age of the brain-injured individual, they will most likely be hospitalized on the stroke victim's floor. You will remember that we discussed strokes as acquired, internal brain injuries. It's my personal opinion that the hospital floor on which I resided was given large amounts of cranberry-grape juice, and so I was conditioned to like the taste during my two unconscious months at the hospital. Furthermore, I espouse that my new favorite smell of bacon was more of a situational conditioning, because I was given large doses of pain killers with breakfast.

Even to this day, when I take my pain medicine, sometimes I smell bacon, when no bacon is present. I had to teach myself not to ask people about the smell of bacon through social re-adaptation. If your loved one experiences unwanted laughter, don't just pity them, take an active role in giving them the words needed to rephrase their thoughts to a more socially acceptable phrasing. You may have to help them see that not always saying every fleeting word or thought is a good thing. Encourage them to write it down, and if extremity injuries prevent hand-use, help them record their thoughts for someone else to write down at a later time.

Recovery may steal away a patient's identity... *for a time*. For as with every cocoon, a survivor will soon emerge.

— Bryan Sisson

CHAPTER 6

SPECIAL EFFECTS

Over the years, perceptions towards the paradigm of disability have varied significantly from one community to another. Literature discussing the history of cultural perceptions towards disabled individuals is scant to non-existent. Ruling cultures didn't want to have to deal with the extensive upkeep and funds required necessitated for the daily living of the handicapped.

In ancient times, disabilities, life-long illnesses, physical imperfections, etc. were all esteemed as below the common norm; and therefore, were termed as manifestations of immorality and demonic influence. Some Ancient Egyptians were known to have found blind people humorous. Ancient Israelites forbade "deformed" and other disabled human beings from entering into the sanctuary of the Most High God. Ancient Greeks, considered the sickly citizenry as inferior (Barker 1953). In Plato's, *Republic*, he recommends that all deformed offspring born to any race should be, "kept secreted away in mysterious, unknown places" away from normal society (Goldberg & Lippman 1974).

If chronic illness or disability is present from birth, in certain folkloric circles even today, the physical faults are attributed to the corrupt spirituality of the parents-of-origin, but most often, especially, the mother. On the other hand, if a traumatic injury causing the disability or sickness is derived later during adulthood, the blame shifts and rests on the individual's actions and/or character.

During the 16th century, however, Christians such as Martin Luther and John Calvin indicated that the mentally handicapped and other persons with disabilities were "infested" with acquired differences because each were possessed by a multitude of evil spirits. Thus, these men and other religious leaders subjected people with disabilities to mental and/or physical pains as a means of "exorcising" the spirits (Thomas 1957). Surprisingly though, this perception of 'demonic possession' still lingers today among many who themselves are uneducated, although most would likely never admit this publicly.

Conversely, I like Durkheim's take on the sociocultural explanation of perceptions towards acquired differences: "the physically disabled are tainted with a profane status outside the sacred space of community" (Willett and Deegan 2001). Why does such a profane status linger so predominately in a democratic society, though? I believe that a large minority of individuals still hold onto the idea that acquired difference is the direct result of internal dysfunction. During my time in recovery, I have been made aware of what I understand to be the idiom, "adding insult to injury." Let me explain.

I remember the first time that someone told me my brain injury was inflicted upon me to correct a spiritual problem. I had been home from the hospital no longer than a month-and-a-half or so, when the mother of a disabled boy we had prayed for extensively came to visit. My Dad had just left the parsonage to attend Wednesday evening services and my Mom and I were sitting in the living room. It was dark outside, wintertime, a dark and chilly February evening just after 7:00pm in Branson, MO. My mom invited her in.

She greeted me cooly, but I could tell she had something on her mind that she was nervous about saying. She moved her hands a lot and kept looking at the floor (as though she were praying) and then in different directions. As far as I know she never visited me in the hospital, but that's not a fair assessment because I really have no available memories during most of my stay inside the hospital.

I had never seen that contrite shape of worried lips directed towards myself before this moment. It's a look that is built on prideful, Christian love, defiant almost; but shaded by a twinge of passive-aggressive, holier-than-thou control. She shared strategies that she had used in talking with God and confessing things she'd done that may have led to her son's genetic disability. She began to cry and my Mom posed a blank stare as if to say, "Why are you here, dear?" The lady continued and offered to "help secure my healing in the name of Jesus," by helping us confess our sins. There were other things discussed about my Dad's recent lack of participation with the church family because he was, as she said, "ignoring the flock to take care of a boy whom only God can heal." I know she wanted to help in her way but didn't have very good interpersonal skills at that specific moment in time. But that look! The one of the spiritual fuss-budget: I will never forget the grimace, because it happened again when I was enrolled at Junior College in the Mid-West..

This time it was on the face of a peer. She sat me down in the lounge of the men's dormitory and shared her estimation with me. She told me that she didn't want my help nor my attention and she wouldn't be borrowing my car ever again. To top it off, she said, "We are *NOT* akin to the same spiritual family, anymore." I do not want to elaborate because I'm over whatever that was, but it hurt my feelings considerably at the time and left me more perplexed than anything when it happened.

After retelling these accounts though, in retrospect, I have seen the bumptious and self-enlightened countenance more than twice, since being released from the hospital. Suffice to say, learning a second time to not wear your feelings on your sleeve is a tad more difficult than the first time. Recovery from TBI will be like living a fairy-tale with a parabolist (your old self: you) constantly narrating the events of day-to-day of the initiator (the new you: you) as people come into and out of their lives. Encouraging a love for writing is one of the best ways to counteract the emotional frustrations that are inevitable in the paradigm of acquired limitations.

Persons with disabilities frequently find their opportunities limited because of social rejection, discriminatory employment practices, architectural barriers and inaccessibility to transport. Social attitudes are significant in that they help scientists determine to what extent the cultural needs of persons with disabilities can ultimately be realized and/or attained (Jaffe, 1965; Park, 1975).

When humans live consciously in the moment, they are unable to communicate easily with humans who themselves seem stuck, pondering the past. I say, "pondering the past," because there is a difference between depression and missing yourself. This is a profound hallmark of closed head brain injuries, but can be experienced slightly by open-head brain injuries as well as any other acquired changes post-puberty. Brain injuries are troublesome for everyone. While counselors would instill that acquired changes may be difficult for most, they would further espouse that this should not be enough reason for sitting around feeling sorry for yourself. But survivors have been transfigured, so it's different than what one might first postulate.

Even though survivors might experience difficulty in getting the brain to be active, we might cause harm if by "treating everyone fairly," we ignore the gravitas of the survivor's acquired difference(s). Especially during the first five years of recovery after regaining consciousness, the conundrum of expectation must be altered commiserate with the survivor's newness.

Your survivor might seem as though she/he is flighty, or not capable of making consistent, firm, and rational decisions. Its important to realize that many of the dreams held prior to the traumatic event are sometimes magnified by their subsequent absence or present lack of attainment power. For instance, before my traumatic experience, I believed that I was going to become a professional singer. Post-trauma, however, I have the joy of living with a remotely-paralyzed vocal chord that tires easily. Its still in the process of getting better, but it's my acquired change. The vocal sounds I produce now are not as pleasing, and the visible non-uniformity of my face provides distaste in some.

Prior to the traumatic event of October 16, 1999; I was envied for my singing ability. It took time to re-learn how to perform simple tasks, such as operating my diaphragm (RME). The voice therapist at Springfield's Cox Hospital is the person who reminded me how to even make noise. She asked me to take in a deep breath and position my mouth as if to say, "Ah." I did as she asked, and she pushed my stomach in… I made a sound. Its embarrassing that such a devout vocalist who had won talent shows and performed alongside some of Branson's best performers couldn't even remember how to speak! For crying out loud!

This inability to make proper decisions promptly and effortlessly may take upwards of twenty years to re-develop and at most, difficulties in being socially agile may persist through life. If you know a TBI impacted individual, for their sake, don't push. It may get very tiresome when they seemingly refuse to make complex decisions regarding courtship or dating to even the most simple of tasks in merely choosing a restaurant to eat. Along the road to recovery, it would be good to practice choices and refrain from demanding immediate abstract ideas, such as forcing your survivor to "act just like everyone else." Maybe your survivor constantly takes the other viewpoint, or defiantly does some simple activity that annoys you over and over again to the point that you don't know whether to strangle or slap them.

An admonishment for such a situation; along this road to recovery, everything will happen again as it did before. Forgive me for talking in riddles here. Subconsciously, the survivor may be remembering doing something as a little child that absolutely drove her/his parent(s) through the roof; but because the stakes are different, and we live in a tolerant society, as an adult, the identical youthful behavior does not meet with a spanking or other form of projected intolerance. Not to mention the fact that for your survivor(s), those memories are decidedly unconscious.

You see, the most puzzling dilemma experienced by your survivor is that, depending on exactly how her/is brain was injured, those social skills are the first ideas to be lost. There are so many friends that I would have in my life today had I known what I know today. True, such a statement can be made by anyone, but for your survivor, the sentence has a deeper meaning that pervades the Darwinian hearted in our Western society, the human mind prefers to subconsciously ignore all the difficulties that not everyone experiences. It takes time to recall the social rules learned subconsciously from childhood. They will get there, but be sure to remain strong, only giving support and encouragement as they reconnect with themselves.

Another facet for understanding is reminding you of the age-equivalence spectrum. Depression in all its forms is unwanted and not fun to experience in any circumstance. Often, the sluggish, confused output of your survivor may be perceived as depression. This is unfair to the traumatized individual, because there is a difference between emotional depression and the mirror of depression. I am no psychologist, but there seems to me a profound identification lacking in the world of depression.

Depending on personality traits and where the brain is injured, your survivor might have a propensity toward anger with you, their family, or loved ones. Because of my closed head injury, I unfortunately am unable to engage in conversations from which personal blame is suggested or to be proven. A survivor's ability to engage abstract thoughts within a timeline of working memory can be difficult, if not impossible, and explicating their confusion to angry individuals, who themselves already hold pre-conceived notions about how the conversation should pan out, can be relentless.

Should any person be angry with the traumatized individual, talking to an unbiased third party first can be more helpful to the situation, but make sure the third party is wholly unbiased. If the said person merely uses a spouse or a friend on their side for the third party, this leads toward the development of hopelessness by the traumatized individual. My theory of loneliness is best termed as betrayal-ideology, because every time the individual questions a relationship, the default understood meaning is that they are unfit to hear the truth from within their original culture. Friends living in the present moment, may find it difficult to observe the handicapped's ability to jump in and out of past-present objectivity.

Once upon a time, an entire civilization was able to ponder actively in the past-present tense. Those great philosophers, whom we revere even today, lived among the Hellenistic Greeks way back when. Since that time of long ago — members of Western society place our ideological heritage as beginning first among the citizens of the Roman Empire; today, we've somehow deleted our ability to speak in the past-present. For instance, it's not normal to say the "friendship was developed this specific day, and thats why we are friending." But all too often, survivors I have met who are championing their injuries possess an innate, child-like mannerism, which causes them to question everything. Non-survivors become increasingly frustrated with us because we seemingly can't just "let go".

Much like a paradigm of being misunderstood; these emotions manifest a backdrop of being unheard. Unintelligent people will call this baggage; but it's really sustained sadness caused by a survivor's inability to communicate successfully using familiar terminology and/or expressions. Until survivors discover personal meaning within their societies, healing cannot even begin to approach completion, in my opinion.

Additionally, what separates closed-head brain injuries from every other injury, illness, and handicap is the impending loss of common-sense, which is after all, the inability to render explicit memory. One of the most perplexing effects of TBI is the undeniable susceptibility for the injured brain to be continually, "mixed-up." One way in which my brain projects confusion subconsciously is through an automatic switching of a pair of first letters. For example, just last weekend, I told my Mom, "You should care your home." She agreed thinking I was telling her to clean her bedroom. I rolled my eyes at myself. I said again, "I meant... you should comb your hair!" This switch-a-roo lineup of a spoonerism is frustrating when it occurs in social situations where acquaintances and/or distant family members think you should already have solutions for toddler-aged word choice problems. How many times in these years of recovery after leaving the hospital have I been asked: "Don't you think before you speak?" I never counted, but it's many, many times. Even though such thoughtless questions can seriously anger your survivor, the knowledge of their survival is made to be suppressed in the social circles. Regardless of what others think though, it's imperative that you come to grips with the reality that mistakes by the survivor are inevitable.

Easy is as easy does. Quite often, humans will always take the path of least resistance. Therefore, we naturally want the path to be easy for our loved ones dealing with the affects towards TBI. We make sure to make their living space clean, neat and orderly because only when everything has its place can the TBI person's mind freely flow. Whenever I've had a tough week and my home gets cluttered, my thoughts also suffer. The injured brain is drastically attempting to make reconnections and a poorly kept bedroom or home will cause a "lack of fluid thinking" to seem even more unattainable.

Through the first several years and even after, TBI individuals are believed to worry constantly. Such a classification irritates me slightly, because it should never have been termed "constant worrying." That would be the description by a non-handicapped person of a TBI-impacted individual's mannerism. From my own experience with learning of classifications and academic evaluations, a more apropos two word identification of this conundrum would be, "constant pondering." I have a very intelligent friend, with whom I lived while in college in Fort Worth. He would always get perturbed a bit with my lengthy remuneration of social situations as I tried to conceptualize if I had truly played any part in other people's perceptions of me. In the kitchen one day he squinted his eyes at me and said, "Dude, you dwell." As we continued going to school, it came to be something that he would say often.

It's a puzzling conception because I don't use that verb except for speaking of what I believe to be a holy presence religiously. The first time I heard him say that I laughed out loud, literally. Life continued though, and I don't even remember what happened; but I haven't seen him in years. It's imperative that, as a community of intelligent human beings, we make separate the views of others towards an individual with a brain injury and our own interpretation of that person. It's a very hard reality to experience, but I came to understand that if I'm wondering, worrying... i.e. dwelling on a person, place, or thing, that is not a healthy environment.

Social situations of varying supposed "drama" often arise between friends, but how much more so when one has an unseen handicap. The brain's propensity for making mistakes is a recurring frustration during the entire 15 years of recovery on the age-equivelence-spectrum. Its unbelievably difficult because people classify as you handicapped and subconsciously don't actually get to know you as a person. The most annoying part of the brain injury is that people tend to estimate you based on where you are, ignoring the fact that over time you will navigate several personality changes before finally leveling back out to who you are.

These past 15 years, I've had moments where I've realized that the ultimate method of rudeness to my ownself is not in what someone says about me, like high school. Its actually the manifestation of signs that they refuse to use a paradigm in which I am handicapped. If anyone says something rude to me, of course I get a little miffed, but if someone refuses to acknowledge the fact that I am operating in a paradigm of handicap and brain injury, any friendship with that person has to come to an end. This may be one of the strangest ideas that unqualified people project willingly onto someone who self-identifies with an unseen handicap. Unbelieving, selfish and quiet rudeness develop awareness of the unfair nature in a friendship. The most rude thing you can do to someone with a TBI is to say, "You look fine to me! Get over it!" Its not that simple.

Prepare for a world of opposites. In high school, I wasn't the one most dated or anything, but I had friends and everybody knew I was a great vocalist. A) I'm NOT saying that we should look back to High School as the age of our generation's glory days! Heaven forbid. B) I'm not saying that High School was better... it was different from who

I'm able to project today. My dreams of the lime-light and stage are not unlike to what they once were, but different from what I'm able to produce today.

Your loved one experiencing TBI has many changes that will be difficult to accept. At each level of change on the age-equivalence-spectrum though, a profound depth in sentience will accompany the individual's progression. This takes up back to the debacle of "accepting" or "disregarding" the brain injury. Even though friends and acquaintances will grow to dislike and possibly disregard your loved one's TBI, there will come a day a few years down the road where s/he will harness long-held dreams and discover new ways of expression with the way things are.

Maybe your TBI impacted loved one won't heal to a state in which they can grapple the magnitude of sorrows concurrent with the effects of TBI. In some ways, it might be easier. If your TBI person doesn't progress to some lofty level of healing... don't ever let them see you cry. If your TBI makes it so that you feel that no one really knows who you are inside... never let them see you cry. The apparent magnitude of humanity's cloud-cuckoo-land outweighs any attainable palpability of plausible dreams that could have been.

Having a big group of friends and getting along with others can be a discouraging task. Before having friends, the brain injured individual has to be able to get along with others on a consistent basis. However, getting along with others is next to impossible if no adherence is given to the injured's brain injury. This does not mean that you need to worry about treating a TBI person differently than you would any other person; but it does mean that you show extra amounts of inclusiveness to the brain-injured survivor.

Time and time again, I have witnessed a double standard. Someone in a wheelchair will start moving through a cluster of standing individuals who will politely move out of the way clearing an aisle for him or her. But when someone parks in a handicapped spot without one of the visible signs, well you can forget any sort of kind allowances. I am not blaming anyone, or suggesting that we make a change; only asking that you, the reader, question your own self-behavior regarding the handicapped.

There have been way too many people write me off as sketchy because I'm a piano teacher. UNFAIR! I'm not pulling wool over anybody's eyes. I'm being honest! Many times, brain injured people, like me, may feel that others such as family find their actions or lofty goals as unbelievable, or taken for granted. This stems from an inability of choosing appropriate words to match social situations and proper understanding of relationships.

If its true that children learn what's appropriate and what's not, how, where and when; what should happen if a youth sustains a brain injury before learning appropriate behavior? Post-trauma, the brain is in social-limbo. The injured survivors will meet with social frustrations in every engagement if there is not one with whom the injured can commiserate equally. In every traumatized individual's scope of human interactions, the mother-of-origin is the key link to amiability, but that's my opinion. As an anthropologist, I would say that someone close to the victim is best suited, as in my case, it was my mother.

For instance, the traumatized individual, who will communicate inappropriately at one time or another, will be shamed by individuals holding to a cultural standard, leaving the injured in complete confusion about why the delivery failed to illicit the same kind of response attributed to a memory of the former self pre-TBI. Many times inappropriate comments and/or gestures often do not stem from the conscious, controlled person known before the trauma. Inappropriateness flows from a nearly uncontrollable conscienceless post-traumatic state. Nearly every time I speak inappropriately since the onset of my injury, they have been words with which I never intended to deliver in the way they were presented. In that moment when the words have already left the mouth though, there is no forgiveness it seems. The world would be a much easier place for survivors if consent was given to brain injuries in the way that extra amounts of kindness is shown to those with visible differences.

Perhaps you've encountered an annoyance with your survivor because they seem to always be hiding from responsible behavior. Again, every TBI is unique, but as for me, I am not in hiding from anything. I used to have a neighbor who would always criticize my every move, and because of his depression he often shared negative views of everything I did. However, to my disadvantage, he had a strong network of friends in the community, and every-time he would talk about me to others, he only permitted his lens of depression to share the things I was doing.

Behaviors by head injury survivors mirror classic traits of Freud's depression, but they are two very different ideas. The main difference can be summed thusly: TBI stems from physiology, and depression stems from emotional wherewithal. The two can be linked effortlessly, but the world must rationalize: a depressed person will sit in their room with windows closed for hours because they're afraid of going outside; a survivor though, may do the same thing, but for reasons common to the TBI. Sunlight can make pain in the skull increase, or perhaps she/he just doesn't know what to do with their life, how to locate the right job, or how to gain enough required sleep to have functioned that day. It is so important that humans do not superimpose their own academic doubts onto another's misfortune.

In my limited experience working with chapfallen teens, I have observed countless cases where youth would have self-inflicted scars, wounds, and other signs of sheer carelessness towards the self. But again! There's a difference between careless treatment of the body, emotions, other people's feelings; and carelessness that happens because of confusion. Unfortunately, for many TBI individuals, its easy for them to become forlorn over the realities of acquired differences, but more so from what's projected onto them by individuals in given social settings. Teach a depressed person that she/he is worthless or unwanted and they just might believe that is so. Teach a survivor that she/he is worthless, and in times of great loneliness, they may very well believe what was said.

In every way, an individual sustaining a head injury will never experience pain in the same way post-TBI. I remember in my 3rd year after recovery, my Aunt came to lead a ladies' workshop at a local church and had one evening free to visit me at my fraternity home in Nebraska. Because my housemates were throwing a party, I had to cook dinner at a friend's apartment, which was a surprise at the time, and I was miffed, while short on prep time. I abruptly shopped and began cooking frozen fish, probably not the best idea for a first time cooking experience with broiled trout fillets. My friend left for work and had placed a fish knife on the counter, and the inevitable happened! While cutting downward, I ended up sticking the tip of the knife right into my left hand, where the second finger joins the hand. I remember moving my finger down like a spout and watching blood flow in an arch above my hand into the sink. I was fascinated, but surprisingly to you perhaps, I was not in "pain."

I tell this story because recovering from a brain injury is quite honestly, weird. And to not put qualifiers on it, a brain injury requires all components of livelihood to rejuvenate. Even to this day, I feel like I'm observing life sometimes, which others try excitedly to bring me in so that I might look and behave more like an included friend or family member in social settings. Sometimes when I haven't had enough time to get to know someone yet, their sort of superficial attempts immediately annoy me, which in turn is then perceived as hostility. Much a contest of debate in my family, I unfortunately have inherited my red-headed mother's temper, and as I've been recovering, it is this anger that has caused relationship problems for me. Here again, not because its just anger that a twenty-something year old should be able to control, there is a deeper TBI meaning to where only a few years ago, I was just learning about this observational trait inherent to severe head injuries.

For myself because of my injury, I'm in pain most all the time. But, its not the normal idea of what someone would write about as pain. Its a dull, sustained throb emanating from the right frontal lobe of my skull, but deeper. I can't say the brain hurts, because the dura matter of humans has never felt or experienced pain... ever. This leads me to consider that no one actually experiences emotions, but that everyone's experience creates the nouns we call, "ideas". In the same enlightenment, bad days, hunger pains, stubbing your toe, breaking an arm - all constructs of pain should not ever be compared to the paradigm of a handicap. For its in the very comparison, that you set yourself immediately apart from the TBI individual. By stating that you've experienced the same type of thing when you were younger, you have implied that you know he/she has "potential," but they have a long way to go. Shame on all of us, who have not taken the time to really understand TBI in the past. Such a conversation would liken itself very well to what might happen if you stated such an immature thought to someone with a visible handicap.

The truth is that recovery from injuries involving the inner-most layers of the human body takes a bewildering amount of time to rejuvenate. This "process" is also paramount in character differentiation, which I have termed here, as the recovery-period from a brain injury. Common injuries, such as the stubbing of one's toe, or even accidentally scraping skin against a hard object, take a maximum of three weeks to finish the healing process. A broken bone, or pulled ligament may take two-to-four weeks to finish very basic healing to start rehabilitating the ligament and/or bone.

For ordinary organs to heal, such as the intestines, esophagus, or skin, the process can last upwards of two-three months. At most the longest recovery time for a basic injury might last up to six months, with residual aftermath during sudden drops in temperature or sleeping wrong cutting the blood flow from the past injury sight. These minor injuries that are predominately just scrapes and bruises are vastly different from the random lottery of TBI manifestation.

Recovering from a broken bone does not require any kind of extra thought or social wisdom to make sure that extra bone marrow be produced for a return to full functionality. Likewise, the internal healing of brain dura matter does not require additional thought or effort, except for the kind of tiredness experienced by the survivor. They may need up to twice as much sleep as they needed pre-trauma, and its important to be sensitive to this, because the life-long recovery process of the dura matter and brain connections happens during deep sleep. If you rob your survivor of their needed rest, you will awaken a serious animal that may lash out inappropriately. Exhaustion is the #1 cause of inappropriate behavior. And the survivors may not understand how very tired they really are, so its very important that the friends and family make sure the individual is getting adequate amounts of sleep.

When I was younger, my older sister was frank, "if you fail at the beginning, try again." This is easy for those who are oriented towards success, difficult for the person who is trying to avoid failure. The status quo in my city for the most successful and intelligent men and women includes a large number of individuals who have never been forced to undergo some unelected physical differentiation.

"The losers visualize the penalties for failure. The winners visualize the rewards of success." This quote certainly calls for wisdom that can be used by borderline, reasonable individuals as they work toward their personal goals. Dr. Media Pump-Fake administers a curriculum with a variety of self-help documents and quasi-educating websites for the masses of untrained people who believe everything they hear.

"May I look upon my soul and shadow.
Bestow me see with eyes that see."

from Chapter 89 of Ancient Egypt's
Going Forth by Day

CHAPTER 7

FRUSTRATING AFFECTS

There are going to be many changes that will frustrate you because of the mere inability for the traumatized individual to control their speech. Because each brain is different before and after the injury, there is no way to clearly predict which specific struggles might affect you or your loved one. However, individuals developing open-head injuries do tend to experience a somewhat different initiation back into societal roles, even though they might be different than the person they were before. Even so, in all fairness, this book is aimed toward individuals who have experienced severe closed-head injury.

Ever since I regained consciousness and left the hospital, I never wanted to have "handicapped" labeled license plates on my vehicle. My thinking even early on, was that if people saw the plates, anything I did would be perceived as though I were mentally handicapped, because as I was learning, there is a difference between mental handicap and brain handicap, in the midst of so many striking similarities. I saw the differences as paramount, though, and did everything within my power to appear "normal." Years later, during this ethnographic summary, I finally decided that one of my first steps towards simplifying life would entail the acquisition of handicapped labeled license plates, despite what others might think. By itself, the reasoning is quite simple, so clear. But this decision was made after a series of encounters spanning years in which I had forgotten to hang my blue-placard (BP) on my rear-view mirror.

The very first time I forgot to hang the BP was when I was attending a private college in Nebraska in 2001, I forgot to hang my BP in the handicapped space at a Target® Store parking lot on a briskly frigid winter morning. After finding unexpected sales on the end-caps, I ended up with considerably more than I had anticipated on buying. But because I didn't want to walk the cart in and out of the store, I decided to embark into the dry- aired cold, carrying all my bags returning to my 1990 Pontiac Sunbird. I tossed the bags into the back of my car and began readying to sit down in the driver's seat. As I began to close my car-door, I heard an elderly man's voice say, "Hey, you! Boy!"

Oblivious to any possible reason for calling out my name, I stood, turning round blankly, "Yes, sir," I said. I beheld a silver-haired caucasian male in a black leather jacket with his shorter wife, an elderly Asian woman wearing glasses and a brown jacket lined with faux-fur. "Why are you parking your car here young man? There are plenty of parking spots open to you; why do you think you can park here? I don't see anything wrong with you." I explained to him, feeling chilled to the bone and offended, "Well sir, (1s pause) you see, (smile) I have (.5s pause) compression fractures in my lower back, (2s silence) and I also have nerve damage to my face," and then I remembered what my Mom always said, but in my own words I told them, "the biggest point about my injury/handicap is that its all in my head." Either from exhaustion of cold or arguing, the old woman scoffed at me and tugged on her husband's coat sleeve, and they entered the store. I remember this moment vividly, because as they left me standing in the parking lot, it began to snow.

There is no fee for forgetting to hang your BP when you show your placard or approved documentation to the authorities. Every time I've taken my placard in to the DMV, they apologize for any inconvenience, and give me one stern admonishment with a smile, "Don't forget next time!" Honestly, its like getting a slap on the wrist from Aunt Marlys and then patted with encouragement. On the other hand though, when parking with a BP and remembering to hang the BP, our culture pervades the minds of its members with societal ranking, in which every law-abiding human must adhere to the norms within the society, or suffer the consequences. In my case, the norm garnering social approval requires a sign, a BP, i.e. a logical handicap that people can see, one of which I do not have.

It's wrong for humans to judge any handicapped person based on appearance or through a lens highlighting socioeconomic status. Even though that statement is upright and seemingly common sense, human behavior of the masses enjoy creating racial paradigms of the us and other. Regardless of a person's political affiliation, skin color, etc, survivors may at times be judged unfairly by those within the culture of these United States. Every single time I have traveled overseas; men, women and even children are more than willing to offer assistance to me based on my handicaps. However, if Western travelers - yes, I am including Europeans, Middle Easterners and North Americans in this statement - (if Westerners) can't see it, they refuse to believe it.

I had a terrible time in the Hashemite Kingdom of Jordan getting my luggage out of the airport. I had traveled there to spend five-and-a-half weeks in Amman with Andrews University of Michigan, USA. I was traveling alone and it was difficult to get help with my luggage because I'm caucasian, young, male and had new-ish looking luggage. This is not an accusation, just an observation. Despite informing the attendant that I could not lift my luggage, he rolled his eyes at me and left my bags on the curbside.

Those rolling eyes, as I learned that day, are not just indicative of US American attitudes. Those rolling eyeballs herald external disapproval by those immediately judging survivors as ambassadors of their self-perceived, but quirky, social justice. I hate parking in handicapped parking spaces because of the angry, disheveled, and comely old people that will verbally scoff, make a production of rolling eyeballs and even mutter explicative syllables as we pass each other in the parking lot.

In June 2011, I attended the "The Lies that Chelsea Handler Told Me" Tour when she and some of her favorite comedians performed at the Verizon Wireless Theater here in Dallas. Chelsea Handler was the social-media guru of E! Entertainment Network's, Chelsea Lately. I was surprised… no, that's not right. I was mortified when curly red-haired Brad Wallack opened the evening's all-in-good-fun performance. He asked the audience, "and what about those people at the grocery store who park in handicapped parking here in Dallas, but don't have anything wrong with them? We have to pause and wait as they do cartwheels to and from the front door!" As I've heard Chelsea say a time or two, "Shut up! Just shut up, Bradley!" But he was not stopped, condemned, or even booed. But please do not tell him because otherwise Ricky Gervais might open a set where he discusses sentence diagramming his jokes to safeguard the comedian's responsibility toward the handicapped.

We must show more faith in our DMV and Doctor's prescriptions before we allow ourselves to be irritated with the system. I cannot do cartwheels because of a right elbow-contracture and compression fractures in the lowest vertebrae of my back, handicaps that no one can visibly see, in addition to my own TBI. Its easy to get frustrated with a world that refuses to believe you.

As a result of that horrible joke, I asked my doctor to help me fill out a license plate form with a printed Winston wheelchair. The change of license plates is exactly the opposite of what I expected. Whether you like it or not, every handicapped individual is perceived by predetermined sociocultural standards from others. From the civil servants who gave me the plates, to the attendants who affixed the plates to the convertible I had at the time, people addressed me with such altruistic sincerity.

I was at the time constantly confused by the wonder-struck, for sure! The moment the mechanic saw the plates in my hands though, he just said, "Oh, I see; what can i do?" For the first time, I felt like a stranger acknowledging my difference. He was so helpful, and I choked. Every time I took my car to that little car wash, they like I was treated. Had I replaced handicapped plates on my car seventeen years ago, my response may have been a bit pretentious. This moment was a strangely honest point of reconnecting and engaging my shadow (my former personality type with) the realities of the changed me as an individual of acquired disability.

One of my skull fractures involved the vessel on which the brain rests; therefore, my hydration reader is now off because my hypothalamus was injured as is usually the case with severe head injuries. In simple layman's terms, it's just a fancy way to say I'm thirsty all the time. Pouring a glass of ice water is a good remedy for post-traumatic headache, especially when the water is poured in front of the hand and cooled, distilled in the refrigerator. However, even after drinking a lot of water, I was during recovery still thirsty. The doctor diagnoses this symptom as diabetes insipidus.

Just as when people must accommodate with aisle size for the person in a wheelchair, allowing service animals for the blind, and various accommodations for other visible handicaps, it should also be mandatory for members of society living with TBI to be permitted water bottles in fine theaters where open containers are not allowed. I am so tired of having to miss the second act of a performance when I really am too thirsty to throw the bottle of water away since bottles of any kind aren't permitted in the relic chambers of certain historic buildings.

Interestingly, I find bewilderment in the sacred truths held by Christian Scientology in regards to human reproduction, specifically at birth of said offspring. I remember most precariously a remark of Katie Holmes as she was preparing for the delivery of little Surrey. "The baby must enter the world in complete silence, otherwise whatever is said at the first moments of life will play in her mind subconsciously, over and over the rest of her life."

I think to some extent when I left the hospital, I constantly heard "he doesn't look handicapped," confirmed tenfold by the scoffing laughs or snide remarks audibly raised by some feeling as though I had wronged them and added to the injustices of their individual lives. Of course, I still hear people say, "you don't look handicapped," but truthfully, its not out of spite or confusion, it comes out with compassion. Something that I have craved from strangers around me, but never received.

Undoubtedly, to help with any of these points, your TBI will cause a need for prescribed medicines, which will medicate not only the problem, but unfortunately your relationships. And in this true confusion-state, survivors may feel shunned or abandoned despite the fact that loved ones are treating them just as they always have been treated. However, for the survivor that is silently, constantly and exhaustingly remapping brain pathways, the second childhood or years inside the TABLÆS, will all be again as it once was before.

In the Walt Disney® family-geared television show, Wizards of Waverly Place, the father figure breaks a crystal ball in the premiere season. He then mutters a pun on a latin phrase, "mcreary, time-reary," and the cast is transported to just seconds before the ball crashed on the floor, and he was able to keep it in one piece. He said to his children that it is a special spell only to be used in the most dire of circumstances. The spell allows the wizards to travel back in time momentarily to solve something or fix an error they caused. Alex, asks, "If that happens to wizards, what happens to regular people?" The Dad grins while pacing the floor, "they experience what they call 'déjà-vu' (Disney Studios: 2008).

I will confess here that I am a Disney fan, and think Wizards® was a tremendous show; but regardless of all that, this is such a devastatingly simple example to talk about what happens with some survivors most all of the time. Undoubtedly, you may hear a survivor laugh out loud or cry in shock, saying that they were thinking of this exact moment while in a coma. When a TBI person says something like this, the important fact is to not get upset or jealous, or even envious! The natural propensity for survivors to feel abnormally high rates of déjà-vu originates from the brain's re-mapping cycle while rejuvenating (Sisson 2010).

It might be that they show signs of anger at something that once made them so care-free, but not because they are unable to do it in the same way; its because that which they produce post-TBI cannot compare to their present abilities and/or talents that existed pre-trauma. For years, I was infuriated by the very sound of my voice while singing, my automatic face contortions and the unconscious remarks and thoughtless criticisms hurled by others. In fact, I still have to consciously remind myself that its okay to not be the soloist, its okay to not be the one selected, its okay to not be the star of the hour or center-of-attention.

At the same time, there are also validations leaning toward the expulsion of those awarded solos or things I've competed for post-trauma, and when the awardees go on speaking of all the musical practices and mentors they've had in their life; I choose to sit still, bide my tongue, and agree with their severe interpretations. At least for me, these past 10 years of recovery, have been the biggest lesson in humility and biding my tongue even when I didn't want to. Recovery is difficult; but it will not last forever. Keep in mind, that even though 15 years may seem like a lifetime at the beginning, recovery along the TABLÆS is merely a process, not a way of life. At the same time though, you must consistently reevaluate your own goals and dreams, cautioning yourself and your survivor to not err on the side of euphoria because "recovered" might never be actually attained by your survivor.

An exacting propensity to be slow can develop over the course within the TABLÆS. Never insist on speedy anything! Whether it be from academic problems to complex social situations, give your survivor room to breathe and think. Everyone involved will assume your survivor is purposefully slow, dumb, or even immature. At times it may seem as though they've given up. Your job is to be the admonishing encourager. A super frustrating example happened well into the trajectory of writing this book! On May Day in 2012, I had walked to a local Kroger's in Dallas, TX.

It's not been my intention to write a book discussing absurd individuals, but this renunciation was too perfect to not illustrate and discuss. I had just taken a self-checkout lane after a gentleman in a wheelchair. The line had multiplied behind me and I took my shopping tote filled with milk, eggs, butter, cheese and some special ingredient's to make my infamous spaghetti. After running through my items and paying via credit card swipe, I began reloading my shopping tote with the purchased items one by one.

Upon realizing that I had loaded the tote incorrectly with eggs first, I wanted to make sure I had saved my 75¢ using a coupon for the secret ingredient. All of a sudden, an elderly gentleman shouted, "Good Lord! We're gonna be here all day if you don't finish up!" I inherited my Mother's angry gene unfortunately, and I bravely held my head high and gave a sincere and opened half smile to the line behind my left. I then purposefully took my time until all other lanes had cleared and others had filled them. Much to my surprise the rude, older folk person came to lane #6 as I was leaving, and he spoke cooly, saying, "Yes, young man, I was referring to you."

I turned inwardly toward the self-register to chortle, "Relax, dude;" turning around, my eyes met with Lakesha, and I exclaimed, "Good grief!" This is why I don't have many friends because I speak my mind impatiently; and my TBI makes it difficult for people to understand where I'm coming from, but hopefully people will read this book and get a clue!

As with most human behaviors, it's natural for a few of life's interactions to cross paths with someone who is a toxic person. They usually don't know not how to steer their feelings of animosity in a direction that is beneficial to everyone involved. Remember to remind your survivor that engaging in heated debates and arguments will do little to rectify social situations. Don't expect them to just someday, "remember". Do not constantly test your survivor or bate them, because if you do this, the judgement on you by higher judicial offices may involve serious consequences.

We must always be careful to not lump behaviors into superstitious categories labeled by demographics. Regardless of traumatization, human beings who might identify themselves as survivors experience a blending of two paradigms in self-expression. In the first paradigm, survivors conceive internally what we should do, who we ought to be and how our social skills should appear to others. For the normal human being, this is identical to the realities of what they project. But in the life of true survivors, the second paradigm is what becomes projected and what actually happens. Let me share a few examples.

I am fully aware that sticking one's tongue out in any setting is distasteful and often considered rude behavior. As a survivor that is my first paradigm of which I've been aware since before I was four years old. Due to my brain injury, I have no control over bodily actions judged by others. Most are slight positionings or quirks which are independent of social etiquette I know to be appropriate for a gentleman of my own age, etc.

My Right Shoulder Girdle

My right shoulder, clavicle, scapula and humorous bones were broken as a result of being thrown from the Ozark Van. During my time in comatose, I incurred a flexioned fetal position. The nurses in the ICU exercised all my limbs except for my right arm because of the broken bones. This led to ossification in my right elbow. Despite multiple elbow surgeries and extensive physical therapy, the teams of medical professionals were unable to free my arm because of brachioplexus nerve damage. My brain still thinks my right arm is broken.

Today, nearly 15 years later, I cannot fully bend or extend my right arm. I also am frustrated constantly by my right shoulder always drawn up towards my head and therefore slightly higher than my left shoulder. In 2004, my trainer commented, "What's that about with your shoulder?" Countless family members, friends and acquaintances say to me, "Why do you do that?", "Can you just relax for once?", etc. I never had an answer for these constant accusations of how others perceive me post-trauma. However, blessings of research endow anthropologists with ethnographic validity!

I manifest in my right shoulder girdle something referred to as Pusher Syndrome. It is an uncontrollable byproduct of past injuries. This syndrome most certainly has nothing to do with what I'm thinking or even projecting. My right shoulder girdle is elevated because of past injuries to the area. Please do not ask me again. It's mildly rude and ill conceived to ask someone why they look the way they do.

In most cases, when physical deficits exist in addition to brain trauma... the individual potentially can "misplace" in a way, their characteristic integrity. If this happens, and in many cases on the TABLÆS it will, the best option or method is to step-back from all social interaction, write your thoughts out, and do not share them! If you're not able to physically write your emotions, use your smart-phone or other recording device to record yourself speaking of your experience(s).

Express yourself as you are now able to record your emotional state. If you think it sounds funny in your head, or when you proofread it; make a note of it and ask someone who you knew prior to the trauma to identify any similarities or differences that occur in your emotional manifest as compared with the perception of yourself, pre-trauma. When you accurately uncover any differences or similarities, there is a high probability you will "find your shadow" from this experience alone.

I know it sounds so weird, but this is part of acquired survival. If the temporal lobes were struck as part of the brain injury, emotions become something that survivors may write or say, but not necessarily "feel". In psychology there is a general consensus that refers to 6 types of basic emotions: fear, anger, disgust, sadness, surprise and joy. However, according the psychology-spot.com, recent research leads with the fact that the uninjured human face can create more than 7,000 different expressions.

Since this has been my experiential ethnography, its my opinion that this basic reality is exactly why we survivors have difficulty connecting, essentially, with the greater culture of non-traumatized individuals. Perhaps its an idiosyncratic trait that is solely mine; but this off-the-wall truth is how I have learned myself interacts within our culture. Some say that its because my filter is off, which I seriously disagree with because if my "filter" were truly shut down, I would speak in a fashion much more aggrandized and peculiarly hurtful. To say it another way, if my filter were "off," I wouldn't experience empathy, sympathy, regret or forgiveness. All concepts of gracious social interaction would be unknown to me.

Prior to regaining operational consciousness along the TABLÆS, consistent filtering is truly shut off: the patient is like a baby or toddler.

This does not mean that the patient should be disciplined in any way as parents might think to do with their child. However, upon the acquisition of the operational conscious state, exciting moments eventuate. The survivor will show subconscious evidence that s/he has attained the next level of consciousness through an expression, a movement or even a realized memory.

I remember the first day that operational consciousness "turned on" for me, while some physicians might technically observe that it was the first time my working memory was triggered. I was laying in my hospital bed after eating my breakfast and drinking two bottles of Welch's® cranberry-grape juice - I could barely speak audibly. Using my spelling board (I couldn't write because of the injuries in my right gleno-humeral joint and elbow) I asked the nurse to help me with the bedside phone. This is also the first recollection that I possess of my entire three-month stay in the emergency room, ICU and hospital floor in Springfield, Missouri.

The day before (I don't remember this, but have constructed it with the help of my medical records), my speech therapist pushed down on my diaphragm and my brain realized the required methods for producing sound. Even though it was barely a whisper, I felt like I was finally doing something that had always been second-nature to me. Even though operational knowledge of working the diaphragm had been rekindled, due to partial paralysis of my right vocal chord, it would be another two years before I would be able to actually speak comfortably.

After finishing breakfast, I called home from my hospital room. As this was before when even preachers had caller ID, my Dad didn't know who it would be. Pushing on my stomach like my Aunt Marlys plays her accordion, I produced the following words… barely in a whisper. "Dad, I want to come home." I could hear my Dad begin crying on the other end and I didn't entirely understand why he had choked up on the phone (keep in mind that at this point, I had not yet seen myself or understood the severity of what was going on… I just remember feeling trapped).

I have always grown so tiresome of people who claim their golden years were in high school; and I wasn't afraid to let them know it. I despise social games incurred by dysfunctional romance. Group mentality is a force to be reckoned with throughout life, but how strange is the discovery that group mentality persists into adulthood. I haven't been the nicest to media outlets, saying they're lame-stream, etc, but the reality is that the farthest reaching outliers in any given situation naturally encourage the most discussion and foster the greatest interest. For journalists this means revenue, for TV Newscasters, innumerable viewers, while internet webpages receive countless visits depending on the sources of gossip and/or dissent.

Part of the reason that we "buy-in" to the spread of media coverages is inversely proportionate to why go to the movies! WE WANT TO BE ENTERTAINED! In the minds of countless lay persons, their biggest dreams are experienced when they recreate emotions as portrayed on the big screen or reported on television. They feel to some extent that if their lives experience what media shows, their lives matter in some twisted way. Survivors are the exact opposite though. We don't do things because we were influenced to think in certain terms. Brain injury survivors operate on a biological level, usually quite distant from the social ideations laid down by Emily Post's etiquette and modern society. "Drama" happens because survivors unknowingly think from a level "all about themselves."

I will always protest that this seemingly awkward and selfish inadvertence is never to be spoken of as immaturity... ever! An all-consumed perspective manifests as the incredible result of recovering from near-death.

Ever so tiny, gradual and calm, allow itty bitty BABY STEPS!!! From the moment consciousness is realized in the hospital or later in the home, a survivor's awareness of emotional intelligence may be perceived differently.

During the first years of recovery, life may seem as though events and relationships are one constant film on the big screen. The projections of other individuals onto the survivor's character may provide false evidence supporting the notion that everyone is consumed with the survivor's brain injury. As the healing progresses, the survivor may become entangled. This is completely normal and will be corrected as the survivor gets closer to their physical age. Society will judge her/im based on their habitual tendency to think everything that happens is because of the brain injury. But the home culture should not be so callous.

It's fitting to remind your survivor during experienced social faux-pas that while their acquired differences take a weighted precedence in their own survival, the knowledge of one's personality encumbered by any number of unique disabilities is truly a secret. The process of ideological transfiguration is a remarkable tool employed by physical and mental recovery against the overpowering backdrop of natural human behavior.

It's one thing to grow up with any and every kind of disability or some combination thereof. I cannot imagine the magnitude in depths of love and patience required by families and caregivers to their young ones when the differences are present from birth. However, from my vantage point, I behold a single blessing for every one of those individuals: they possess no sociocultural knowledge of anything different.

Those who gain any number of acquired differences later in life (after the age working memory introduces itself to consciousness), are afflicted with the sociocultural knowledge of their respective difference(s). What I mean to say is this, emerging again onto the social platform is difficult for every survivor; but how much more so when certain acquired differences are visibly present!? Of course, it makes sense to just tell the survivor to grow up, accept the cards they were dealt and get over it. However, while many will say these things, only a few can truly understand the complexities required to produce confidence from this core of acquired disability.

Every memory of social ability directs survivors to expect different cultural outcomes than the ones they actually receive. The shadow-self is always expected, no matter how long the survivor is distanced from the trauma; but the acquired disposition of the sociocultural perception toward the one surviving is received. Snickering, rude comments motivated by jealousy and entitlement, questions regarding BP parking, blatant disbelief in head injuries being as bad as the survivor says - these and many other quandaries can lead the survivor to utter sadness, loneliness and fear of rejection. The hopelessness encountered at this stage can lead the survivor, depending on their personality, to make a conscious decision that they will deny any and all effects of the brain injury and operate as though nothing is wrong. I would err on the side of bad advice if I told you that this can be avoided. It will be difficult and the survivor's actions may be completely unfamiliar to you; but I believe that it's an essential component of meeting one's person with acquired differences. True confidence returns after time spent in ignoring the brain injury.

You can try to explain the mystery of ideas to the survivor, but understanding that everyone's pain scale is subjective may not help curb the basis of the survival problem: understanding how to use your physical person to achieve obtainable goals. You can also attempt to direct the survivor to audio-books or radio programs that retell or exemplify the dangers of being self-obsessed, of course at the emotional level they're presenting to be the most comfortable. On this side of the traumatic event, your role as parent, guardian, spouse or other caregiving person is not necessarily to instruct, discipline and/or punish using methods commiserate with time-outs, stern speech, or the age-old myth of spanking. Your discipline style should encourage the survivor make repetitive mistakes. At the same time, don't just leave the discipline-making decisions up to your survivor's medical staff. Ask your survivor's brain injury doctor to refer you to someone that can actually help your survivor and family increase knowledge in working through the recovery process.

If the injury eventuates during adulthood, as caregiver, your purpose should be reminiscent of an old friend always offering sage advice using a healthy conversational style. In this way, a parent, spouse or loved one allows the injured brain of the survivor to you systematically return to correct line of thinking in your home, family, city, country and/or world view. Each time the survivor remembers, they get that much closer to their first selves. You will now from a renewed attitude, an old behavior, or if they can formulate understanding, express the realization in some meaningful way.

I will allow others to tell their stories of personal experiences during recovery; but I want to take a moment to describe the eerie uneasiness I experienced during my recovery to consciousness. It's my hope that even if it helps you understand your survivor for even just one hour, my own story can help you guesstimate the sincere, but so very awkward, jumbled thoughts survivors can experience along the beginning year of the TABLÆS.

Even though I awoke in November of 1999, my family brought Thanksgiving dinner to my hospital bed, and I had been using a spelling-board to speak to friends and family… it was not until December 16, 1999 that I concretely knew where I was, or at least remember thinking I knew exactly where I was. The morning of the 16th, I had a few nurses and therapists holding me down and attempting to bend my right arm. I still remember looking around the room and seeing dazed persons walking short distances with weights, two or three doing sit-ups on various colored training mats, an older male was assisted to the fountain and several officials dressed in white cloaks were taking notes on clipboards. In my mind, I had no idea how I had been captured, but I knew something was wrong. I opened my mouth to scream and nothing came out. As I began writhing and twisting my legs, the "scientist" in charge, Angela, said, "Okay guys, it's not going to bend today."

A guy on my left laughed out loud, saying some explicative, and the male nurse sitting behind my head said, "Man, you're just too strong; but don't you worry, we'll get it to bend tomorrow."

I could not figure out what was happening and got a little freaked out. I didn't know anyone in that place, but I deducted, beyond-the-shadow of a doubt in my pre-conscious traumatized state that after converting to Judaism, the Nazi's themselves had captured me. My head hurt, my back hurt, I couldn't even move my arm and when I made it to the water cooler, I can't even begin to describe the horror that filled my chest. Slowly, I reached my left hand to my cheek and with my index finger drew a sweeping line from the side of my forehead to my mouth and traced my lips. Eli! Eli! L'mah sh'vaktani? I did not quote this because I thought of myself as Messiah, but I really had no idea what was going on and I looked to myself as one forsaken. I remember the weighted awe of this moment... How am I here? Who are these people? God Almighty! how am I in pain? What happened to my face? And when I realized I couldn't audibly speak, I was flabbergasted! No sound emitted from my mouth as I balled to heaven about the realization of my left eye-patch, drooping mouth, and right elbow cast.

I saw some nurses gathered at the doorway to the great room and Angela called me over, "Bryan!" she said, "You forgot your medicine at breakfast!" She gave me a huge, rather hard-to-swallow pill and after returning once more to the therapy table, my memory grows dark.

Every time the human brain creates a new memory, a new pathway of dendrites between neurons is formed. Nearly two years before this experience, I had been a member of the fast-track, Humanities class at Branson High School. We had done extensive research, class projects, and studied various literatures concerning the experiential knowledges of the Holocaust. It wouldn't be for about another month until I had been home for a few weeks that I would consciously understand what had happened and why I had been there.

As a parent/guardian/caretaker of survivors, it's imperative that you be active in your estimation of the survivor's placement along the TABLÆS. Engage with the survivor in discussions to remember their shadows. To this day, there are a few who are unable to actively discuss the changes manifested by my new personality type. It's difficult for them to think they could comment on said differences without hurting my feelings and without themselves being overcome by the sadness they experienced when discovering I was in the ICU in a comatose all those years ago.

The difference between a right word and the almost-right word is the difference between lightning and a lightning-bug.

— Mark Twain

CHAPTER 8

FITTING OR APT

In November of 2013, I had the honor of publishing my first book. A Kirkus sponsored, post-production review of that work brought to my attention that which I already knew of my post-traumatic writing style. In their critique, they professionally judged my writing style as, "clumsy," and a bit too influenced by clichés, quoting one of my opening sentences, "To know where one is going, they must first know where they've been" (Sisson 2013). I had attempted to pen my ideas in that work free of any awareness/excuse of brain injury or survival paradigm. In retrospect, however, how can a bird write of fish in the sea, without subconsciously phrasing aquatic-jumping with the experienced awareness and impact of air above water?

I do not mean to belabor the point here, or retaliate towards the reviewer(s). There is a time and place for everything. I only share this as proof that your survivor post-trauma will be bombarded with continual and sombre reminders of how others perceive the survivor's acquired difference(s). To some degree, any acquired uniqueness where memories of a life pre-trauma persist, introversion will become hitched to the survivor's transfigured personality.

Culture mandates that a person a) speak from experience or knowledge and do so credibly. Society enforces a strict coherence to certified proof of adequate training. Your survivor will come to learn that a) they're unable to manifest prompt and timely recall and b) depending on any visible injuries, they may be judged by cultural perspectives as unable to have ever been able to perform the skills or tasks explained. What's the most shocking and detrimental to the psyche, is the frustration implied by society. Regardless of any proofs of past brilliance, natural talents, etc. society automatically deems those skills and past accomplishments as deliberate falsehoods intended by the survivor to create drama when they are merely attempting to remain true unto themselves. Even though its predominately subconscious and completely unintentional, human behavior compels us to think, "If and *when* I see it; then and only then, will I believe it."

Life on/inside the TABIÆS will be tiring for your survivor; but you can help them make it through. It's important for parents/guardians/caretakers to be aware of the clichés that may manifest in the mind of the survivor. In this chapter I'm going to walk through some constructs that must be allowed for every survivor of severe brain trauma to fully comprehend, and ultimately accept, any known acquired difference(s). The gut-wrenching heart-break realized by the shadow person is unlike anything I know of associated with contemporary philosophy.

1. "I'm brain dead."
2. "I can't do it."
3. "Maybe I'd have been better off to have died."
4. "Perhaps I should self-medicate."
5. "I'm not sure I want to live anymore."
6. "I don't know what you want me to do?!"
7. "I don't know how."
8. "I misplaced myself."
9. "I refuse to love this person."
10. "This body is like a prison."
11. "My spirit left me here."
12. "Is it all really worth the effort?"

A discouraged and perplexed spirit is radically different from a depressed character, as per my experience at least. Time after time, when I heard survivors of sTBIs speak at the community support group held at Oak Lawn United Methodist Church, my heart would be filled beyond capacity with compassion for the older folks that talked about their own experiences with counselors and various medical professionals. Their stories of being shuffled between any number of counselors led them to ultimately refrain from seeking counseling.

In my personal ethnography, I've been shocked again and again at how psychologists, counselors, doctors, etc. don't know how to exhibit proper boundaries when discussing some ideology of perceived loneliness experienced within the TABLÆS. Maybe my problem should be directed instead towards HIPPA or various help-lines, but I don't want to be negative. A well-meaning survivor can talk about ANYTHING without fear of retribution; but if the natural question-and-answering session eventuates concept(s) of the afore mentioned eleven phrases, the socially constructed dynamic of the professional relationship changes.

"Hold on now," the counselor may interrupt. "How long have you been thinking about suicide?" They are required by law to ask this; but for true survivors within the TABLÆS, these questions are a natural step in transmutation towards the acceptance of one's identity in possession of acquired difference(s). I'm not trying to fill this book with suppositional evidence and opinion, but this has been my ethnographic experience inside the TABLÆS vacuum.

I have *never* thought about killing myself >.< I will further admit that I was pretty much clueless as to how a person would actually commit self-homicide anyways. That is until my first counselor at UNT went through a suggestive checklist so he could confirm I was most certainly NOT thinking about that method of suicide.

There may come a time when your survivor will present what sounds like suicidal ideations. To a great degree, though, caretakers must realize that just because something looks and/or sounds like major depression, it's not always that, every time. If these phrases are uttered in the hospital, medical officials and social workers are required to make note and report using various channels, regardless of whether or not actual suicide gestures and/or attempts may actually be present. When in the home setting, though, don't be afraid to listen to what the survivor is saying. In my personal ethnography, these phrases are often summated to express complicated truths that should have been discussed more freely and not trivialized or disciplined away.

"I'm brain dead." Obviously the picture depicted by this phrase denotes an offensive idea when used to describe the actions of others as being blindingly inferior to the secular norm. But what if someone states this about themselves? It's seemingly contrite with a garnish of self-pity… isn't it? Not quite. Let me explain.

To the survivor, they might be highlighting uncontrollable social misunderstandings, felt or perceived, resulting from the presence of brain trauma. Any social misgivings, verbal mistakes and even certain cues manifest differently than what we conceive internally to physically produce or verbally express.

I remember the first time I said this, when my family took me to the funeral of an old friend back in our hometown. I think I was still wearing my eye- patch, which always was a source of embarrassment, and I remember seeing a few old friends at the church. Once everyone was seated though, my mother began to play the organ. When the speakers began going to the podium to give their regards and blessings of the deceased; it seemed as though everyone was crying, mourning or deeply grieving. And as I myself became overcome with sorrow over someone I had known and respected several years prior, laughter began bubbling up from my lungs. Not the kind of hardy-har-har laughter evoked from a stupid joke; but genuine laughter like you would hear on the set of Jimmy Kimmel. Numerous people began turning around to look at the back pew, and I knew from the dozens of stringent and furrowed brows, I had to excuse myself from the sanctuary. I had no control... I couldn't make it stop.

Climbing over a few people seated in my pew, I clumsily made it to the center aisle and opened the large doors of the sanctuary. Once outside, the door closed louder than I had anticipated, and I just went and sat in the bathroom because that was not me. I don't think I'd ever been so "disobedient" in church since I had been a baby. I could hardly bare to show my injured "pirates'" face out there before family and friends again. Utterly bewildered, I froze.

After the reception had been in operation for awhile, I finally emerged from the restroom. Finding my parents, they helped me get some punch and a nut-cup. My mom, who had been playing the organ, asked me, "Are you okay?" I think this was the only time I ever replied, "I didn't mean to laugh, nothing in there was funny. I'm sorry, but *I'm brain dead.*" A couple of girls in earshot giggled at this, but my Dad (out of love) sternly said, "Bryan, your brain is fine. Don't talk that way!" My mother voiced, "Pa-," as if to say, "Paul;" but stopped mid word as members of the congregation approached the table. I think I brought up the ideology of why it was bad to term my mistake in that way on the long car-ride home. But I don't remember ever actually talking about it.

"I can't do it anymore." Social media and countless human beings who themselves are struggling through self-evaluation and self-help concepts will hate this one. When interacting with survivors of brain trauma - if you truly desire to show self-control - people ought to harness their knee-jerk reactions and engage politely. When survivors say they can't do something, listen to what they're trying to say.

Despite presenting oneself like a toddler along the TABLÆS, many older survivors maintain the learned knowledge, but they will be clueless for the first few years as to how they initially required said knowledge. Because the injuries incurred allow me to manifest a young man without acquired differences, hundreds if not thousands of people perceive me as some depressed curmudgeon.

Pre-trauma I was instructed with heavy doses of "Yes, you can", "Keep trying", "Cheaters never win and quitters always lose", etc. What people fail to realize is that survivors are entrapped in a kind of hell where the known physiological responses of second nature require work post-trauma. When I would say, "I can't do it anymore..." I'm not telling you that I'd rather give up or heaven forbid, end my life. Especially during the first 5-6 years along the TABLÆS, survivors of severe head trauma develop conceptual reason as prepubescent Tweens. The output is confusing to everyone involved because while survivors are enduring the coma-catch-up and behaving, as many will tell you, like children, adult survivors are intrinsically perplexed because our child-like innocence is juxtaposed with hormones and adult thoughts.

More often than not, when survivors tell you, "I can't do it anymore," what they mean to tell you is, "I can't function like I did pre-trauma. Everything is different." For myself, pre-trauma I could barely whisper into a microphone without the audience applauding. This is my truth..."I can't do it anymore." Post-trauma, if I go onto a stage to sing a solo, the minute I open my mouth, at least one person says, "What's wrong with him?" Being aware of human behavior with regards to my acquired differences doesn't make me depressed. Granted, of course, it has made me quite sad at times, but that's why mourning and grieving must be allowed for every survivor. No one can do it for her/im, which brings me to the next statement.

"I miss me." Awareness to one's own acquired differences cannot be realized without an understanding of the person one was pre-trauma. To put it simply, "To know where one is going, they must first know where they've been" (Sisson 2013). Native American populations are full of diverse personalities and wisdoms. To the greater academic world of professionalism which focuses on concrete, verifiable reality; anything that appears to be a spiritual, internally motivated concept cannot be proven, so why waste time trying to figure out what this individual is saying. If it acts like a duck, sounds like a duck and eats like a duck, it's identifiable as a duck. If it sounds weird though, it probably is weird.

The run of the mill populace is going to judge your survivor to a point where they may be afraid to be themselves in public. Just like when a child learns that touching a hot stove will burn you; survivors realize that if they put themselves in certain situations that make them sound or look funny to others, they eventually learn to avoid the situations and/or individuals entirely. Due to nerve damage on my left cranial 7th nerve, my facial nerve; when I smile freely, eat food or even sing publicly, the gold eye-weight in my left eyelid causes just my left eye to close momentarily, inspiring individuals without boundaries to conceive that I'm winking at them! What's pitiful here is that the people who think they're that great begin avoiding you. If you bring it up or apologize, society perpetuates that you were thinking of winking.

As a survivor saying "I miss me," I am informing you that I have to work at social interaction in a way that Bryan David would never have needed to do pre-trauma. I have learned to modify my appearance somewhat, but the reality is that nerve rejuvenation is like watching grass grow. Mix that with a bit of impatience and it may seem to your survivor that "Life just doesn't seem worth all this brouhaha."

Frustrations encountered by survivors of acquired differences are, in a word, lugubrious. Of course, there are better ways to phrase complex ideologies, but at the very core of the human experience, "Is life really worth all the drama so many buy into?" No! because people should do unto others as they would have done to them. Most however, are entirely too focused on their own personal advancement to allow for the paradigm espoused by the TABLÆS.

My parents did a great job of allowing me to recover, but I know so many who did not have enough time allowed within the TABLÆS and were subsequently pushed out of the recovery nest too soon. If professionals, media, family members, etc. (i.e. society, in general) insists on promoting the idea of significant, quicktime recovery, the subgroup of survivors may never convalesce.

Although we all must first learn about religion, or its antithesis, from the nuclei provided by our families of origin, many adopt their own families of choice to help shape their personal beliefs. Eventually, every person, regardless of their society and culture, observes, reacts and produces based on their experiences with random individuals ... those random personalities, who actually by accident are too numerous to be counted or even named, are those which I like to call, the family of chance.

CHAPTER 9

THE FAMILY OF CHANCE

Time spent with the family-of-chance kindles the perceptibility of the survivor's ability to express her/him-self in some way that is remarkably different from that which was exhibited by the survivor's shadow-self. Usually the family-of-choice consists mostly of any number of individuals who have little to no knowledge of a survivor's shadow self. Many times, non-professionals are unaware of affects caused by the ABI. In several cases, it's among the family-of-chance that the survivor's new personality is created with the presence of any acquired differences.

First thing's first. These are the top explanations of a few arguments gleaned from my own ethnography of living with a TBI.

1. *Grow up already!* Never, never, never tell your survivor to grow-up. In my own life, I find this to be cardinal rule #1. Nobody likes to be told they're acting like a child. Strikingly though, several factors inhibit survivors from modulating onward toward an adult-like and/or more 'mature' set of social behaviors.
2. *I can't tell if you're talking or if that's the TBI.* Seriously? This is a hurtful one that you will undoubtedly hear on the road of recovery. Shame on the ones that ask such a question.
3. Understand that '*letting go to move on*,' and, '*remembering the trauma*,' are in fact two, extremely different ideas. This is another difficult definition debacle, but the real heart-of-the-matter is found by "moving on" because one remembers, or at least that's

what worked for me in my recovery. TBI survivors have to remember the traumatic effects in order to operate successfully as members of society.
4. If emotions take the best of you, do not merely respond; remember to ask, "*What did you mean by that?*" I cannot stress to you the importance of this simple question, and the grief/drama you will save both yourself and the TBI patient by adding this simple question.
5. *Aren't you over it yet?* Although seemingly previous, this question strategically places a lesson commensurate with every brain injury, big or small. Pain is a very real occurrence with most brain injuries. Severity and frequency depend on the inverse of the individuals' traumatic experiences.
6. *Write things out before you speak to everyone.* This sentence made it in to the top 10 hateful things you can say, but it's covered in my personal story in chapter seven. While for some it may be true that speaking before a crowd can make your heart aflutter, it's also true that for the traumatized individual, there are thousands of signals firing in the brain simultaneously which never amount to appropriate outputs. It's difficult because the memory of what one is able to do is different from what happens. If either of the parietal lobes were injured in your loved one, and they never had trouble communicating their heart pre-TBI: you'll seriously have to exude more patience than you ever thought necessary or imaginable until they find the ways with which to remap their brain.
7. Some suggestions of things NOT to say to your friend or loved one with TBI at any time post-trauma, regardless of recovery phase on the TABLÆS.
    A. Don't use body language to judge yourself or your TBI victim. This is not fair to anyone involved. This includes facial twitches, body jibes, and random movements. Read on and be sure to refer to the dictionary for definitions as well.
    B. So you never lost your intelligence? (RME) Closed-head brain Injuries are unique, because despite being classified with stroke victims, who have a brain injury from blood vessels inside the brain, a closed-head brain injury is caused by an

outside force. Throughout my time in recovery and even to the present day, people are clueless because the handicap is hidden.

C. So I'm supposed to give the TBI leeway to do whatever they want? We all have to make personal changes, it's called being human! Whoa there, Senior Expose! Truly, I have to tell you; if you had an ounce of humanism, you would never think to ask such a stupid question. This is highly offensive to me as a person, and even more so as I speak for most TBI recovering individuals. It's very true that the pump-fake media is to blame for an incredulous imagination.

D. Hurry up|you always have this pause to where you make it awkward! Okay, in all fairness, please remember that the brain never completely rewires to a state that allows the traumatized individual to completely meet their expected placement on the age-equivalence spectrum. #10 is the outward appearance of #7; i.e. the perceivers' ability to allow the frustrations they see in the traumatized.

E. "I choose to believe what my eyes and ears tell me." What happens when we allow only our eyes and ears to believe the things people say.

F. "Why do you look like that? Why does your body do that? Do you know how you look?"

G. "I'm so glad you can park in a handicapped spot close to the movie theater!"

H. You look fine to me.

I. Grow up already! You're worse than a child. I will see your full wager and ante up on this one. This is ridiculous to me that we live in such a judgmental society! Well, at least that I do in Dallas. My goodness, I constantly refuse to engage in arguments because I know the absolute truth. Say, for example, we recall a recent return flight to DFW. I was traveling with individuals I knew and was having trouble walking off the plane ramp, accidentally blocking a child from her mother, and an attendant called to me, "Sir, you're going to have to remember that we all need room to exit the plane." So I slowly stood to the side of the ramp.

I chose to share these quotes from my personal story for a number of reasons that could provide further insights into the annoyances I've learned to cope with the rudeness people naturally speak and project because truly, they just don't know any different way to behave. Although, go through these scenarios with me one more time, supposing I had a seeing eye dog or a wheelchair. Survivors do not want special treatment, we do not deserve an easier life over anybody else, but we crave the ability for people to understand us. The one person whom I would say had been my truest friend through the entire trip, asked me what the woman had said, and I asked, "Why, does it matter?" He smiled and said to me, "Because you looked upset and she did too!" What on earth am I supposed to say?! How do I control that moment of utter disbelief in humanity? In my mind, I fought back tears even though my aqueducts were dry and never spoke of it, until now.

I was not angry, I was trying to listen to her and give my respect, however, the woman was on my right and my friend could only see the left side of my face. This is the premiere example of people only taking my face at 'face' value. I could understand why the woman was irritated because she saw the side of me that looks like I'm perturbed and laughing, but my friend, who I have told of my facial injury and TBI, didn't even take into account that he was looking at the side of my face that always looks dejected and grumbly.

Perhaps your TBI individual is free of the facial/frontal lobe double syndrome, but regardless of all my story, if you tell your TBI-impacted person to grow-up, the emphasis should be on ideas for improvement, not just a random accusation arising from your impatience. When people say that life resembles a box of chocolates, mistakes arise from choosing to stay up late, mingling with the wrong crowd, arguing the wrong side, accidentally lashing out linguistically — these methods of retaliation are inane and take place during the pubescent Jr. High years. 1) We already have established that sTBI can cause memory-loss and amnesia; 2) you've seen or heard of your survivor during the initial stages along the TABIÆS, as they relearned common tasks, such as mastication, swallowing, walking and the leu; 3) you've likely witnessed your survivor(s) relearn to identify colors, numbers, the alphabet, shapes; and depending on their achievements pre-TBI, be reminded of reading, writing, and even arithmetic.

Its only fair that you also understand that readapting abilities for beneficial social intercourse will take many months to a number of years. I mean that when survivors suffer from trauma to the frontal lobes, it's far from easy to just readapt as if, in my case, I should feel remorse for not believing in the miracle that saved my life. My Dad once speculated that if I had, I wouldn't experience frustrating struggles with others. Furthermore, I am not writing these answers to shame or continue familial arguments, but only to present my own understanding of this trajectory we call life. Please remember that no matter if they want to punish or disown you, the work you personally have done in recovery is an astonishing achievement in its own right. Depending on the severity scale of the TBI, its important to remember that just like a toddler, you have gone once more through the stages of emotional intelligence.

Perhaps your survivor incurred their head injury while at work, as I did in college. Maybe they suffered a mild concussion in high school on a sports related activity. Brain trauma also might have resulted from your survivor's gracious defense of world powers standing against terrorizing behaviors overseas. Regardless of how your survivor sustained their head injury, and to what severity subsequently followed, survivors do show difficulties in producing age-equivalent/appropriate behaviors. During the initial weeks of recovery (time spent along the TABLÆS) the changes in speech, coherence and cognition will rapidly increase. It's good to remind your survivor that the head injury may cause her/him to respond like a child in the midst of their adult peers; thus appearing to them as immature. If you were normally quiet and reserved before your head injury, you may find yourself the opposite person in your post-trauma reality of acquired difference.

In today's culture, it is more than acceptable now then ever before to divorce a husband, wife, partner, lover, etc. on a whim or "just 'cause." It is highly possible that veteran survivors returning from war may meet their loved ones with mild resentment. Possibly, they're going to say, "I didn't sign-up to deal with this problem or help you grow up all over again," or "I didn't fall in love with who you are now, I fell in love with the old you." Others more religiously leaning might say, "You're possessed by a demon, and unwilling to change!"

This is a fallacy, and Appellate Judges ruling in this sort of court hearing ought find blaming TBI for divorce as wrong, but to be fair, this is merely my opinion. Human beings may surprise me by working together and communicating more effectively than has been my own experience. While projecting my own ideas onto a society might be considered, anthropologically, writing faux pas, proving culture learn from my experience attributes purpose for this, my ethnography.

Importantly, you ought always remember this fact: a brain injury, like a handicap, never modulates, or heals to a natural state. If you're reading this book to understand a loved one, he/she will never completely be the same person you knew before the traumatic incident. If you're reading this book to understand a new friend with a history of brain trauma, it may seem as though the person is constantly changing their opinions, or never quite the same person from day to day.

You might write him/her off and assume that they're depressed or "just weird," most likely you'll term the individual as "the one causing drama." Because after all, if you can't rely on someone to always behave a certain way, or spouse the opinions identical to the first time you had a conversation, common sense would say, "that person is lying, and treating me unfairly, why should s/he get special treatment?!" Stop right there! before you read any further. Such thoughts are unintelligibly unfair. I'd like to help you understand why.

It has often been explained to me that areas of impact during a traumatic event involving injury to the brain causes those portions of the brain under the skull to be destroyed. However, because the human body is a miraculous creation (or self-grown development), its ability to replicate and reprogram itself is a good example of real-time evolution.

For instance, a serious point of impact in my experience was the frontal lobe on the left hemisphere of my brain. The frontal lobes help the face manifest emotional communication, and the left side produces symptoms associated with sadness, grief and loss. Since one of my skull fractures was on the left side of my head, I'm not able to display visible signs of sadness, etc.

Because the brain is in a constant state of "remapping" when engulfed by the TABIÆS, sadness manifests outwardly with the physiology available. In my story, sadness created joyful laughter due to the fact that laughter is controlled by the frontal lobe opposite the location controlling tears. Even to this day though, I can have inappropriate emotions, trying to keep laughter to a minimum. I have the ability now to control it successfully to some degree, but it remains that the culprit is the brain injury. Sensitivity to social situations takes time. Don't be pushy with yourself or your survivor(s).

We've all heard the expression, that the human brain is like a computer, but I don't believe people really think it through often enough. If a computer is exposed to trauma, i.e. a chip containing several important program options is removed, the computer will only be able to operate with what's available. In similar manner, the brain is only able to function with the areas of the brain still intact for the first few years.

The central area of the brain controls sexual behaviors, "in the back of the mind," and deep to the skull. Unfortunately this is the one area of the brain that is normally left unscathed in closed head injuries. Whereas before the accident, the individual may have displayed more conservative interests or even been a wallflower, she/he will most likely exhibit opposite characteristics surrounding this human necessity post trauma. It's as if some primal palate colors the mind's ability to act and reason using natural discourse within their society.

When you witness oddities in your survivor, such as their sudden discussions on unfamiliar viewpoints, as the caregiver it's important to not permit culturally based stigmas onto the survivor's thoughts or actions. Wait until a time when you know for certain that pain medicine has recently been administered to speak privately about the curious views or new ideas espoused by the survivor. Try not to judge the survivor too harshly. Remember that the traumatized victim is wrestling with recovery from an injury to their identity. Wait until a time when the two of you are alone in which you can discuss the new point of view.

By speaking of the viewpoint, attitude or behavior at the instant that she/he produces the said attitude, you're actually confronting the individual, albeit in love and respect the way you always did. So you may be expecting the individual to solve problems and situations resolving conflicts the way she/he always did, but sometimes, the unconnected mind will take over, and the survivors will feel as though they've been thrown into a debate of who's willpower and stamina is more steadfast. To say the least, these struggles can be overcome, and the traumatized individual will learn unique methods pertaining to their specialized injury for controlling their emotions; but this remapping and relearning of social etiquettes cannot be rushed, nor can it be taught as it was in childhood, because adulthood is inflicted with hormones.

TBI presents an almost irrational series of mistakes, reminders and new mistakes to which cultural norms have no say; save the learned father or cultural elder, who mandates a general feeling toward the survivor stating that they are childish, immature, or lacking in common sense and decency. I hope only to help people understand what sometimes happens inside the mind of those TBI-patients who cannot yet speak for themselves. This is not a war about who is better, worse; right, or wrong.

Brain injury does not make a person lose their character, but as its hidden from everyone, including the survivor, for a time, severe head trauma can result in transformed personality. A traumatic injury to the brain does not make survivors confused about their feelings or emotions - survivors often don't realize in the moment how to express themselves. A brain injury's cause is not identical to the manner in which a stroke victim might lash out at a family member. As a result of TBI, the survivor might struggle with anger issues until they have the wherewithal to accept their acquired difference.

This process is what I refer to as the transfiguring personality, or simply, transfiguration. It's not as simple as just accepting the unique differences. Survivors must be allowed to make a series of behavioral mistakes, hopefully within legal reason, and come to understand the differences that may even be invisible to themselves for a time. Each opportunity for recognition of the acquired difference(s) is not just a simple checklist of things a survivor can or can't do anymore. Every new internal revelation of the acquired difference also bares within its awareness, a possible multi-layer tier of mourning the lost self. This can become exaggerated if negative comments and actions by others bombard the survivor's self-perception.

This multi-layer tier of mourning is unique for survivors of head injury. Without the presence of a strong support system, the survivor may literally lose themselves. This does not mean that they lost their way, are apologizing or saying some remorse of past action. Seriously, they are meaning to say, "I lost my true identity at the moment of trauma and I'm confused about how to recreate myself under present circumstances." However, the display of mature concepts in such a long sentence is not available in the minds of children. Survivors may emote the complex idea but especially if temporal injuries exist, what some might express is innocently child-like from their physically older self.

I know in my own experience I didn't communicate with the suave demeanor of my pre-trauma self that could give an answer for just about anything. The initial moments after awakening from comatose are super sensitive for the survivor, but in most cases the working memory will not even be something to think of or expect. Consciousness is not just eating fruits produced by some forbidden tree… it's a process in the paradigm of survival. It's not like every day for the rest of our lives we continually reawaken from comatose. At the same time, however, some may have trouble firing up their working memory.

I refuse to allow my own head injury to overly handicap me in some debilitating way; but it's like people are always thinking I just want a free handout because of some injury from which I appear to have recovered. Heaven forbid! Physicians, leaders and managers understand that life is difficult for all of us, including the non-traumatized; but how absolutely ridiculous are the people thinking I *want* others to identify me as handicapped! Others judge me because they think I desire to park in a spot closer to the grocery door, or think I wanted to take tests for college exams in a testing center in an office of disability. There are others who think that somehow I'm achieving all these things unfairly… or by lying.

Pre-trauma, many survivors would never ask for more time to test, or quieter spaces to complete homework. Granted for myself, those attributes may have helped me score my 3.75 GPA in high school. But post-trauma, for survivors there is no question. We have to have accommodations because our brains are too busy with achieving survival. And this is perhaps one of the hardest conclusions you will need to help your survivor accept post-trauma. In 2005, Jill Briscoe originated a catch-phrase in her publication, "The New Normal." I've had two or three individuals approach me during my time in TABLÆS, and they always said, "Let it go, everyone is having to accept a new normal to function properly." This idea of blind acceptance of my personal new normal was rather depressing to me, because my survivor-hood is not entirely like me. Acquired difference makes survivors different, not stupid. We're trying so hard to be like the people we manifested pre-trauma — ourselves — but its not that easy.

Every time we get closer to figuring out how to solve a problem due to our injuries, life throws a curve ball and because survivors sometimes work slower, it's like watching flowers bloom in real time. Yes! watching this and later reflecting on the series of events is difficult to observers but embarrassing to survivors who may act as nothing happened. Its best for caretakers to not allow their perception of head injury to control the survivor's activities.

Although such a process may be frustrating to parents and guardians, it's best to behave as though the injury is not there. If you stand and watch expectantly, you can't tell that anything is going on, but if you come back after a day or several hours, you do see beneficial changes sprung to life. This is why family members and close friends must not place high requirements on survivors! If you do, you're libel to push your survivor(s) away or even halt her/his recovery process on the TABLÆS. Be patient; be careful; be wise.

If you ever have trouble with society's perceptions towards your brain injury, talk to someone. Don't go it alone if at all possible. You'll find that having this injury encourages countless moments of frustration. You're likely to become confused pretty often and have to ask others to explain the same thing over and over. I know this injury appears inscrutable, but qualified professionals are making strides every day. I don't know if it will be in my lifetime, but their is coming a time when people will respect the gregarious inadvertence of our globalizing economy and social structure will make common sense the awkwardness imposed on survivors.

Bryan! Dude, just let it go; give it a rest! Stop hiding behind some idea of disability that limits you, you look completely fine. (laughter) RME This was said to a family member when everyone thought I was still in another room and unable to hear. If you are experiencing the aftermath of trauma and have heard words like this from family and friends, I'm so sorry. Jealousy is a tool of the worst kind and so difficult to combat when you're doped up on pain medicines and anti-depressants. If I could, I would give you the biggest hug as though your bestest friend because I understand the pettiness and ridiculous hurtful words that people can say. As my counseling mentor told me, "I can't do anything about the stupid things people do, but what I can do is help prepare your heart for hearing malicious stupidity."

If you've just begun your Craniamatic line and the TBI is new, I want you to know how very full your life can and will likely become even without the use of your previous skill-set and talents. Recovery is going to require every ounce of energy from you, survival is not a walk-in-the-park. The process can take a significant amount of time, and it may teach you more about patience, kindness and self-control than you ever thought imaginable.

People are going to be rude. It's natural group theory mixed with a bit of evolutionary process that will make people say you are immature, petty, unable to grasp cultural identity, manifest true forms of friendship and loyalty: they will even think that you don't understand modern ethics! Like me, you may be surprised at how chapter 2's recovery phase never seems to come to an end.

The frustration you might experience may surprise you about how quickly human beings can change their minds regarding what is acceptable. If you are religious, be prepared to encounter the lunacy of the extreme far right who may tell you to your face that your injury is the result of unrepentant sin and/or demonic possession. If you are an atheist, be prepared to meet with extreme far-left people that will tell you they can heal you using magic and herbs.

Quite likely, at some point along the TABLÆS, it might feel to members of your family, community or work culture that you are purposefully holding back (going backwards). If you know that people in your group of acquaintances are projecting these ideas, then in my opinion, there is only one option... Remove yourself from said cultural influence.

In religious homes around the world, its common that mentors and parents will tell their youth or students that a means of keeping the mind "clean," is by preventing impure into your mind. Some make stringent rules on what is acceptable for children by putting walls up to PG-13 & R-rated movies, making sure that the internet is password protected and ensuring delivery of biblical education in a communal church family.

It may seem rash to some, but what is the way to keep negative projections out of your survivor's recovery process on the TABLÆS? Remove any and all permissible contact to said individual(s) or group(s). If you feel like you can't keep up with the circle of friends, religious group, or other sociocultural groups, try to speak with them a few times first. If, after providing ample opportunities for them to apologize or just accept the reality your brain injury survival-hood should beckon you to stop their nonsense by just walking away. I left family-of-origin out of the suggestion, because if it is a family member being rude, I don't want you to just walk away from the group of humans on earth who should be bound to love you no matter what.

"So its just something we have to live with, regardless of personal values, we just have to accept that you're not able to meet our expectations?" When family members are used to having control, it may happen that the survivor of brain injury will have to walk away from an incepting family. I'm so very sorry if this is your reality, because you may experience a kind of loneliness only portrayed in such classic novels as Jane Eyre or Dracula.

This was the hardest thing I've ever had to do. However, the answer short and sweet, is "yes, your expectations are not important in my biological fight for life." Stroke victims, while not always, are usually of older populations. Its easy to take care of someone who you know deep down believes in right and wrong, and raised you to be the person you are today. The unfortunate incidence of survivors of head injuries however, I believe is helping to create a whirlwind of suicidal ideation and behavior. Parents and spouses of survivors do not want their children exposed to the survivor's attitudes/behaviors. The problem here is that loved ones don't realize their particular survivors feel the exact same as they. I am so very exhausted with having to explain myself in this way, but yes, survivors require the same love and respect that is given to stroke victims!

When a survivor of head trauma is forced to communicate on the spot, they may say things they don't mean. Receptors in the brain take forever to restructure so that a task so simple as speaking a thoughtful, uplifting answer, takes forever to relearn. This is not the survivor's fault! It is a problem originated by closed-head whip-lash of the brain.

Instead of ignoring what a survivor says, give her/him the chance to rephrase their words at a later time when they've had a few weeks to mull over their answer. Do not immediately judge what is said, that is not your place even if you're the parent-of-origin. Instinctually, it would make sense to shun bad thoughts and/or actions, but just because something unwanted might transpire, adequate time must be allowed on the TABLÆS so the survivor might truly develop the overwhelming comprehension of their acquired differences.

Although dependent on individual traumatic trajectories, TBI is a lifelong change. Please don't make the mistake of thinking that you know how the traumatized feels or that you've been in their shoes, unless you too have experienced a closed head brain injury of similar severity. Otherwise, just be nice and give them space to redevelop. 1) Try not to push, 2) don't over project and 3) don't let societal perception influence your behavior toward your loved one.

The traumatized person will most likely use somewhat nervous habits, or physical ticks as they relearn to communicate. The words they wish to express are at times not instantly available at the moment ideas are conceived. If this happens, just be mindful that the brain itself is twitching as it figures out how on earth to reconnect. You should smile. Don't look away. My TBI doctor of ten years always told me in his medical office, "The brain injury is like a thousand glitches constantly firing."

In many ways, its as though SuperMan is attempting to mend the broken electrical cords to restore electricity to Metropolis. Due to the complexity of the human brain, we find the singular reason about why the brain injury takes so long to heal. Almost like President George Bush in the early 2000s, "No Neuron Left Behind!" Our brains have to awaken each little neuron, of which normally sum upwards of 100 billion. For every neuron, there are anywhere from 1,000 to 10,000 synapses (electrochemical pathways) through which our brains are capable of sending signals all over the body. There are more synapses in the human brain than stars in the Milky Way.

When conceptualizing the sheer scope of recovery ideology from a traumatic brain injury, its a good idea to remember that the blood vessels of the brain if stretched out flat would measure a distance of 100,000 miles or more. In addition to these most basic, any injuries that happened simultaneously with that of the brain are being restored. This provides a backdrop to the peripheral successes of the signs a person can see in which the survivor is, "getting better."

I say these things to admonish you never to use signs inherent to body language the same way you might with a random, everyday individual. TBI patients, especially in their first years, should never be judged for body movements they use when they speak. *Body Language for Dummies*, will tell you that when a person shifts their eye-gaze to the left or right, if speaking to you in private, are most definitely lying to you. But oh! the wrongs you may cause the survivor by using such rules of communicative behaviors.

Trauma to the brain keeps the body moving even when they're not trying to say anything. Those 1,000 glitches present in the survivor's brain subconsciously manifest in what appear to the untrained observer as a myriad of body twitches: eyes fluttering back and forth, awkward smiles, frowns, eyebrows and winks, child-like giggling, etc. In the body's ability to re-map itself, every muscle is in a rapid state of re-structuring, reconnecting and rewiring. Problems understanding even the most subtle social cues, producing correct emotional signs and even being able to listen, may be something survivors will have to live with for the rest of their lives. In my own experiences with TBI, I have had people misinterpret things I say, things I do, and reactions to countless in-discrepancies as though I'm hiding something, or I'm out to get them, or like I'm somehow designing some hidden agenda to take their social position or deceive them! NOT SO! I want only to be a friend, to whoever you may be.

The brain takes at least 10 years to remap and rewire to catch-up to the actual physical age and between 15-20 years to match socially. If you ask a TBI person to just get over their injury, it's possible that you are asking them to forget a part of who they are inside, or even externally, and act like those dreams were never attainable in the first place. When I lived in a downtown, Ft. Worth apartment some years ago by now, I was accused by some girl as having always had nerve damage to my face and the "old folks" in Branson must have pitied me. I wouldn't understand for a few more years at this point, that spiteful redactions of internal frustration are actually events of unwavering projection.

I know, I know — "don't give up!" But such awareness of oneself is accurately the frustration of the brain injury… at least for a time, especially at first. Prior to the injury, there was NOTHING that could stand in my way. I don't write this to project self-pity or garnish empathy from others more fortunate than myself. I share this because a TBI is more different than anyone's modern sense of disability or injury. Its peculiar, I'll give it that, but it can't even approach the bar to which I hold my shadow.

Since my facial nerve injury was so severe, I'm unable to form vowels using the proper methods of singing. I will be the first to tell you that Jane Munsen-Berg would put her hands casually over her ears, shake her head and say, "No, no, no!", if she heard and saw my face today. In my post-traumatic state, I have had to devise internal arrangements using my tongue to produce vowel sounds others can make with just their lips. To be sure, this ends up looking quite colloquial and unrefined to anyone seeing me perform.

"Can you say it again or rephrase what you're telling me?" The especially difficult part to remember is not asking only others, but yourself as well. The truth comes out in point number four, because no matter what you learn from this book, this paragraph point encapsulates the very essence of trauma to the brain. As a human race, we are not fittingly adjudicated towards extending patience to all people(s). I am not advocating for molestation, pedophilia, perversions, rape, or any other vile behavior when I say TBI is a social handicap.

There is an entire realm of disabilities that the disability associations are just barely beginning to uncover, in my opinion. It is my personal belief that by listening to all people we can accomplish the truest form of compassion, something severely lacking in this world. For instance, if we want to dream big... Jill Briscoe's new normal for acquired difference would educate everyone correctly on disability etiquette. That is society's handicap, they just *don't* know or wish to understand.

"Aren't you over it yet?!" The simple answer short and sweet is 'no.' I'm not sure any survivor fully "gets over" a closed-head brain injury. Most of us can't abide the grown adult who talks about high-school achievements as their most arduous points of career. I know I certainly never wanted to grow old and be that "type," as I termed it then, "of dissatisfied grown-up." Most of the people I heard talking of past achievements were either college drop-outs, high-school sweethearts, or druggies just released from prison trying to identify with a youthful crowd.

I have this religious brother who is always very patient with me, until he starts to feel bad for something he said to me, or just gets entirely busy thinking about other things. He's one of the smartest people I know, but there is this thing he does that absolutely agitates me. He'll say things like, "Oh, well, that's just where you are in life; I understand because I was there too." I asked him, "You've had a closed-head brain injury, too?" He told me, "no." Don't be pompous to others when attempting to be kind.

The fact is that its okay to stand up for your invisible handicap, and it should not garner feelings of hostility by people to whom you explain its existence. Normally, busy bodies automatically assume that you're telling them you deserve preferential treatment because you're better than they are; and nothing could be further from the truth. Its only that we ask for the same kind of respect you show others with visible handicaps. Don't belittle and think that we see ourselves as better than you. Realize that survivors are trying so hard to fit the social mode, and it's exhausting, because fitting some mold requires huge amounts of energy from us! We can look the part with great effort, but survivors won't necessarily always feel the part.

On the road of the TABIÆS, you may find that your survivor might prefer to be a bit of a recluse. It's easy for friends and family to observe the survivor's new personality negatively. because its easier to sit in solitude than it is to try and keep up with social intercourse. When the traumatized individual shows signs of ongoing sadness clearly: never smiling or laughing with everyone else, crying, portraying a dejected, somewhat pathetic character, always thinking people are out to get hem, or even questioning your relationship to per, it is of the utmost importance that you reject every impression projecting from your character onto the TBI patient.

Every brain injury and recovery process: 1) takes an infinite amount of time and 2) diverges distinctly from every other TABIÆS known to humankind. If the frontal lobe was traumatized, emotions may appear to be forced and insincere. In many instances, survivors have the feeling that "they don't know how," to smile or be constantly upbeat - which for the record is completely different from someone who is depressed. A person with post-traumatic stress disorder (PTSD) believes in any number of super-imposing factors that hold power over them to keep them from smiling and being upbeat. For the survivor of head trauma though - because of medications (discussed later), focal injury, and a misplaced sociocultural guide of etiquette - the truth of bewilderment naturally persists in a state of confusion. Not as depression per se, but as active-awareness of the shadow-self.

I'll say it another way, TBI does not mean depression. When a survivor is forlorn over the fact that they used to be better at something pre-trauma, its because they actually were. The concept of remembering the trauma is so important. If you act like nothing is wrong, you'll likely cause unforeseen problems elsewhere in your body. Allow yourself to grieve the loss of your initial personality - your shadow - for a time. Grief of who you knew will not be a life-long struggle.

For some reason, though, present society does not allow survivor to mourn publicly or articulate this reality. Truth be told, every single person is different from whom they would have been if their life courses had remained in sync with their hopes and dreams. Where an injury to the personality is concerned though - i.e. for the survivor - the authentic consciousness is different.

During the 10-15 years that ought be allowed for modulating through the TABLÆS, the hopelessness resulting from the ever present shadow-self may be acutely realized. For this reason, family, friends, acquaintances, etc. may hold the survivor of acquired difference(s) to a comparative scale with which they believe to be of sound judgement. The subjective nature of comparing one's experienced trauma to another's perceived trauma is like comparing apples and oranges though. They're different.

I will make mention that negative emotions always have the potential of being received by others as, in a word, explosive, when emotions of great magnitude are expressed by survivors in real time. In this same realization, though, sociocultural dysfunction lurks at the very core of every frustration. Many people will tell you that depressive behaviors cause survivors to be enamored by past experiences. In fact this idea of depression can become so severe that people can and will not allow the survivor to develop even an ounce of happiness in the present; because they hold on to whom the survivor was before.

To this end, I've been the brunt of social dysfunction on several different occasions during my time spent on the TABLÆS. The most important lesson to learn from these experiences is that silence is the survivor's strongest ally. Whenever I would share the memory of a past experience from my life pre- trauma, people would engage my stories of reminiscing. But when motivated to share the talents described or produce suitable evidence of having experienced life beforehand, I often was greeted by malevolent mutterings and whispering judgements that I must have a misguided perception of reality or be a liar.

My ethnographic experience has shown me that survivors must consistently be the bigger person. Survivors must carry dissatisfaction with others silently. Interestingly, human societies have forced people of all races, ages, persuasions and sizes to keep quiet about disgruntled realities or unfair treatment by family members, friends, acquaintances and even strangers. Remember at the beginning, "If I can witness it, I will believe." If the immediate perception by others is different than you expect and/or desire, it's imperative that you adopt silence as a means of maintaining group cohesion.

This realm of group theory encourages us add qualitative meaning to the present display of quantitative statistics and demographics present in many medical circles today. Advocating awareness of symptoms, epidemiology and mortality is not enough to irradiate the social confusions experienced by survivors.

One of the main reasons for the traumatized person's dejected character is due to the life-long headache that accompanies a trajectory post-brain trauma. It has been my experience where each point along the skull was fractured or fissured will create pain if not treated long-term. Trauma stages may relapse and cause further pain if a survivor experiences whiplash of the brain in any of the following ways: through identical traumas to the original TBI, riding on a roller coaster, bungee jumping, sky-diving, snorkeling and any number of reckless activities; 2) forgets to use a closed air pressure space, such as convertible or jeep with the top down driving very fast, a space simulation machine and/or 3) engages scuba-diving with an oxygen tank.

In Dallas, my neighbors often equate an individual's ability to be low-key as a person's level of grounded-ness in themselves or even some method of judging an individual's confidence level. That is to say, that someone who is actually care-free "should be able to ride a roller-coaster and not hold any of us back!" In this, survivors can face toil and trouble, because the minute they say, "nah, you guys go ahead, I can't." The masses automatically view the sentence through their own depressive lens which may translate to them as though the survivor is saying, "You guys aren't being very safe, I'll stay here because I'm better than all of you." When that couldn't be further from the freaking truth!

You guys go on ahead, I can't, should be able to mean just that, but in my experience, it just causes gossiping to spring up between people you think are your friends and those who are mere acquaintances. So, for that reason, I just don't do risky behaviors anymore, because human society rarely exhibits appropriate boundaries. This is very sad to me, but its the truth.

It has also been my experience that the first two points of the list cause the fissure remainders to hurt more and has stimulated a reddening of my left eye. But its the scuba-diving that is the most painful. In 2005, I had the opportunity to travel to the Kingdom of Jordan to help with an archaeological dig of the Madaba Plains, just south of Amman. During one of my free weekends, I traveled with colleagues to Aquabah, Jordan where we spent the day at the beach of the Red Sea.

All of my colleagues decided to go scuba-diving, and I didn't want to be lame, because so often I have to pause and not engage. I had been swimming lots of times at my YMCA back home, but I remembered how my jaw and face popped when jumping off the diving board. Therefore, I decided to just get some scuba gear, but not the oxygen tank, thinking surely it wouldn't hurt to go snorkel with my head just a few inches beneath water. How incredibly wrong was I?!

After swimming for less than 30 seconds, I had to just give up, because the moment I submerged my head underwater, the displacement pressurized the brain and sent sharp lines of pain through my ears. I remember thinking to myself, "I can't do that anymore," ultimately laughing at myself because I'm aware of how people can go crazy in their evaluations. Survivors may feel as though an acute sort of vacuum hose is placed over each ear producing a compression tone and blowhole that radiates from beneath the brain through the ears. The feeling was uniquely painful for me. Be sure to talk about new activities with your neurology advisor before going out on a limb!

What do you have to take medicine for? Pain is an abstract notion, not a concretely fixed commonality. If a person has to ask why another takes pain medicines or anything prescribed by a medical professional, for that matter; as a survivor, keep in mind that you are not obligated to reply. However, social games people play may force an answer out of you. If you perceive individuals bating you for some answer, "I have a brain injury," should be satisfactory; but in many cases, that just adds fuel to the fire. Our differential hiddenness used to be so under-reported and misdiagnosed that humanity threw survivors to the wolves, literally, or stoned them.

"So you never lost your intelligence?" Seriously?! I bring this point up for your reading pleasure because the joys of most closed brain injuries happen to be free of intelligence loss. In fact, partly because of pain medicines, concentration-aids like Ritalin®, the mind becomes infused with being able to think clearly. At least in my case, growing up I had been faintly jittery because I was made fun of relentlessly. School work took so much extra time because I didn't know that I could have used mood elevators or concentration prescriptions, but hindsight is always 20/20. It did take me around two years to fully recover enough to where I was able to think and reason at the level of a college-aged freshman, but I am so thankful to my family-of-origin for the loving care they afforded for me during my time along the TABLÆS.

God made him that way. Whoa there, Sally Boo-Boo; watch your mouth! You do not know what you are implying to the survivor's circle of consciousness when you say something so brash. Acquired differences may be appear to be physical handicaps present since birth, but survivors have not always been survivors. This complex point is strictly for survivors of severe brain injuries. Just because you answer a question of why someone looks the way they do; you are ignoring the character of the individual. Remember to acknowledge the acquisition of the difference in a tasteful manner.

Oh, memory, the mind's eye is of the brain.
    For the heart — it remembers not;
  And that same heart — can never recall.
    It feels, it hath felt — that is all;
      Still that *feeling* — when unforgot,
     May yet be a feeling, felt again.
       All such joys, my *brain* renews,
       But my *heart*, will never choose.
Altho' I might *recall* what I *felt* of old, I
     barely feel that, which I *recall*.
      Replete — now this, the change,
    So often, this puzzle *feels* so strange!

                        — Owen Meredith
                        Traditional Hindu song

CHAPTER 10

LOCATING HOLISM

Gael Lindenfield maps out an emotional healing process that is good to consider. Her book aims to help you improve your personal healing skills, in order to better cope with emotional hurts and challenges. She developed a journey through seven stages to recovery: exploration, expression, comfort, compensation, perspective, channeling, and forgiveness. Her very own path has proven its effectiveness in handling day to day trials and more ardent struggles.

Allen Elkin gives insight into the steps necessary for de-stressing your psyche and creating happiness in life.

1. Relax: You need to know how to let go of tension, and be able to relax your body and quiet your mind.
2. Eat right and exercise: Be careful about what you put into your mouth. Engage in some form of physical activity regularly during the week.
3. Restfulness: Try not to burn the candle at both ends. Get to sleep at an hour that ensures that you can get enough rest.
4. Openness: Learn the difference between what is truly important and what is not. Put things into perspective and don't be consumed by trivial matters.
5. Don't get angry often: Avoid losing your temper, but if you do become angry, try to remain in control of your anger so that it doesn't become destructive.

6. Get organized: Feel a sense of control over your environment. A cluttered and disorganized life leads to a stressed life.
7. Manage your time efficiently: Know how to use time effectively. Be in control of your schedule.
8. Create a strong social support system: Spend time with your family, friends, and acquaintances. Have people in your life who listen to you and care for you.
9. Live according to your values: Know what is important and what is not. Make sure your goals are significant and worthwhile
10. Develop a good sense of humor: Laugh at life's hassles and annoyances. Be able to laugh at yourself, and don't take yourself too seriously.

During the recovery phase from my own severe brain injury... yes, the entire 15 years; holistic emotional-healing remained unattainable. Certainly, I had moments when I would be able to match my old personality and create happy memories with family and friends. At the same time though, the ability to do so was completely dependent on a host of elements inherent to the acquired=reactabilitative-in a word, complex stratified pseudo sphere. The theory is represented in pictorial form on the following page. When used in tandem with the TABLÆS, I believe the subsequent analyses may provide rationality for quantifying Darwin's survival of the fittest as naturally excluding survivors from engaging in their cultures and their overall placement in societies. Philosophically, its a bit like comparing apples to oranges. Holistically, though, awareness to differences that make individuals unique bares insights into the treatment realized by individuals living with handicaps, regardless of whether those differences are visible or hidden.

Keep in mind that individuals with differences from birth or early childhood cannot necessarily conceptualize the realities of living life without any difference from the normalized status quo of humanity. Secondly, please don't apply this theorem to your survivor/patient verbally or as a means to manipulate a given situation. Just a reminder that the entirety of this book is to be read as though a road-map to understanding the recovery process experienced by survivors of severe head trauma.

Although my mindful education is in applied anthropology (Sisson 2007), my lifelong hobby is archaeology. In 2005 when I completed my Bachelors degree at UNT, I gave myself a graduation gift in the guise of summer school class credit in Amman, Jordan made possible by Andrew's College in Michigan. During this international summer school, I became quite familiar with archaeological inquiry and discovery.

When beginning any archaeological expedition, professional diggers "fence" in the area to be studied with small stakes at each corner and run twine or fishing line 2-3 inches above the ground's surface around the sectioned-off square. Every few inches (determined beforehand by the site supervisor) the archaeologist will make certain to affix small, square pieces of paper with numbers written on them in numerical order and record any findings citing their locations within the square. Each layer that is numbered, is then referred to as a "locus."

I do not wish to make generalizations, but it is my opinion that depending on where the brain is injured, our mABIs siblings incur a higher level of psychological frustrations post-trauma since the recovery time allotted the traumatized is recognized as requiring only enough time for the physical, visible injury to heal and dismissing emotional traumatic effects as secondary and superfluous injuries.

As I volunteered my time on the Reservation, I discovered that youth who made the strongest efforts away from suicidal behaviors were the ones to whom I shared empathetically, "I hear you." We cannot use one culture to address the needs of another. Although, thanks to linguistics, psychology and human behavior, I think we can focus in a bit more. If anyone reads this that can effectually create changes in the treatment of all brain injuries, I implore you to pass these observable paradigms on.

Although head injuries heal over time, every survivor of their own must mind a brain.

—Bryan Sisson

CHAPTER 11

WHO IS THIS PERSON?

Dissonant experience does not appear with every unique rehabilitative trajectory, but I know that just an ounce of resonating truth felt by others is indeed good for the soul. The primary truth I hold to be foundational for every survivor's success is not just summated in the survivor's abilities to withstand or endure pain. It doesn't stem from the placement of skull fractures or even, to a certain degree, on the presence or lack thereof in perceived miraculous cures. From my own personal ethnography, my opinion tends to support the amount of allowable time spent in the second birth as the most critical element impacting survivor wellness.

Perhaps the most paramount difficulty experienced by the survivor entails the somewhat overbearing paradigm of child-like mistakes created by ourselves in social situations. Although few and far between, there do exist brain injury professionals, who comprehend the nature of this reality. Unfortunately however, for the survivor, these doctors, nurses and therapists do not always commingle within the survivor's social circles.

Earlier in this book, I described the moment I first remember seeing myself in the mirror. I do not completely have words that can come close to describing the shock of what I was seeing. My facial skin tone was taught and healthy colored except for a sunken feature with my right eye. My left eye was covered by a plastic covering that looked to me like a pirate. I have never had rhinoplasty or work performed on my lower jaw, but the left nostril seemed deflated. But before Angela had called me to the therapy mat, I traced the left cheek as a method of investigation.

"What is wrong with my mouth?" I thought. When I had taken a gulp from the water fountain, water had fallen from my left side. Not like a few drops, which is normal for most people, but a major portion. Even though I had taken a lengthy gulp, when I straightened my head I remember how dry my throat felt. Then that's when I saw it. In retrospect, it sounds like something of Lewis Carroll, but I could not wrap my head around the devastation I saw peering back at my right eye.

I haven't seen Angela or any of the medical staff in Springfield since we moved away, but I'm fairly certain that I was not supposed to see myself yet that day. I guessed at it being December 16, but the truth is I don't have a recollection of the day it happened. I do know, however, that if that was the day my working conscious memory kicked in, it makes sense that I was released about one week later on December 23, 1999.

Sometimes, in the very first two years of recovery, I experienced unquenchable moments of sorrow and hopelessness. I can still have great sadness creep up on me if I dwell, am overly psychological or even hear derogatory remarks concerning my disabled, that is, "different," personality. Rationally, it makes little sense to even engage in the self-thought banter of what might/could/should/would have been. Emotionally, though, acknowledging and grieving over the known shadow person is essential to the paradigm of wellness and social recovery.

By no means was I considered Mr. Exceptional because of my average, Midwestern, boyish looks or preppy ability to keep white fabrics spotless. But I used to get so down on myself when those within my sphere-of-influence would mimic the half-baked facial expressions I cannot control. I would always scream in my head, remaining outwardly as though I were clueless to their contorted faces, "How do you suggest I express myself with a damaged vocal chord and facial paralysis?"

It's likely that if your survivor(s) were outgoing and expressive prior to their traumatic experience(s), the ideology of decorum may superimpose an aspect of introversion onto their realized personalities. This singular difference bares potential in causing frustrations with people known prior to the trauma.

- "It's like they're completely different!"
- "This is not the person I married!"
- "You cannot act this way and continue interacting with our family."

- "Did you just decide to give up?"
- "You're not doing anything to help yourself."
- "What's wrong with you?"
- "You've become someone I don't even know."
- "You're over it physically... stop! Get over yourself."

Believe me when I tell you, "I've heard it all." It's hard to believe that human beings can be subconsciously cruel with an intent to help some situation. That which will catch you and your survivor the most off-guard is when someone known to be morally upstanding explicates trash talk to keep themselves or their families free of a brain injured construct, namely, your survivor.

Firstly, the Western world must function in the knowledge that non- handicapped and handicapped paradigms are different. Individuals ought not use one to identify and explain the other, but so often they do. They believe they possess hidden knowledge because of what they accomplished.

Secondly, well, introducing this second paradigm is difficult to even suggest because before typing here, I rationally and fairly have always believed that human beings ought not be judged by others according to any types of demographics or labels. I want no person to read this section of my book and judge it as promoting racism, sexism or anything else frowned on as illegal. Within the same keystroke, however, people should learn to acquire kindness for interacting with anyone they deem as different.

I may not necessarily engage in requesting political change at capital hill, but if you are dedicated to your survivor's well-being and newness, I trust that you will plant this peribology in the minds of others. Common sense would tell you that this truth is not only Constitutional, but intended by the forebears of these United States. Introducing an idea such as 'capism should not be performed lightly.

I don't care that my life is different. Although, there is a strange and muffled cloud that can descend when behaving with your own personality and ignoring the the effects of head trauma. This is precisely why my stance concerning the self-help phrases - "accepting the new normal," "letting go," or "allowing nature to take its course," "giving it to God," etc.- remains firmly resolute. These phrases accomplish good work with helping specific cultures of the world's population combat a host of emotional depressions. Their presence is necessary in counseling and helping members of society phrase their trajectories. I'm merely requesting professionals and various caretakers with family members of survivors conceptualize the impressive magnitude by which the survivor's reality is strikingly opposite. I'd like to provide a few examples from my own ethnography at this time to back up my opinion.

Giving it to God

The first example comes from my mother's ethnography of the grief-stricken parent. After I had awakened from comatose and stable enough to be moved to the neuropathy floor with stroke victims, I still was not using my working memory. My parents were trying ardently to resume continuation of shepherding the flock of Tri-Lakes Christian Church in Branson, MO; nearly a 45-minute drive south of Springfield's Cox Hospital. My Mom played the piano every week, led choir and my Dad was the preacher. About the Sunday before Thanksgiving, after service, my mother was approached by a visiting couple.

"Excuse me m'am," the middle-aged male with glasses said. "Is it your son that nearly died several weeks ago?"

"Yes," my Mom said while organizing some music on the piano. "I'm Janice."

"Pleasure to meet you. This is my wife Doris and I'm Frank. We have your family on our prayer-list at church."

My Mom smiled. "Thank you. You know, we were so scared, but God is blessing him and our family so much right now. Prayer is so powerful."

Looking to his wife, Doris seriously nodded her head while tightening her grip holding his hand. Frank turned back to my Mom. "That's why we're here, because we desire to help you pray."

"Oh, well thank you. I'm blessed to have you pray with me for my son." My Mom smiled and bowed her head.

Doris half-chuckled as she reached to my Mom's folded hands. "No, that's not quite what we mean, Miss Janice. We're seeking to help you pray more fully and make sure you're praying for the right kind of healing."

My Mom kept from frowning, but asked, "I'm not completely sure I understand what you're saying."

Frank spoke up, "What Doris and I are trying to say is that from the comments made by your husband at the pulpit, we feel led to inform you that your theological perspective might be incorrect. We approach this subject out of deepest respect, but we're concerned."

My Mom realized that most everyone had exited the worship center. "Can you explain what you mean a bit more, please? I'm still not quite sure I completely understand."

"We've seen this type of thing happen before to members of God's flock. When parents confess their sins to God's chosen people, The Lord reveals the spiritual cause(s) of why this devastating injury afflicted your son."

My Mom was shocked and speechless.

Doris filled the silence kindly, or at least she meant to, "But if it's not you or Paul, the disability is likely the result of some sins enacted by your son." Frank put his arm around Doris' waist and said,

"That's right."

Doris continued, "You're aware of the reality that total recovery will never befall Bryan until someone confesses what they've done, aren't you?"

Trying to be sweet, my Mom said, "No, I don't think that's right, he wasn't driving drunk or recklessly; the accident was really no one's fault. If you wouldn't mind, Paul wants to take lunch up to the hospital today, but your prayers are appreciated."

"Oh, Frank, you were right," Doris half-whispered holding her hand over her heart.

Frank took hold of my mother's elbow compassionately.

"Janice, the fact you're getting defensive tells us that Bryan's condition may very well be the result of something you did specifically. Don't worry, you can tell us, because we aren't part of your husband's flock." Frank and Doris then laid their hands on my Mom's shoulders (as though preparing to wage a holy war to reconcile my mother's consciousness—my words, not Mom's).

"Franklin," my Mom said while looking at the floor. "Doris," my Mom smiled at her. "Do you remember when Jesus taught others concerning the causes of disabilities?"

"Of course, Janice, that's why we're here. We've been noticing some similarities between Bible characters and your family."

My Mom half-laughed, but harnessed her frustration coolly.

"I'm glad you remember the Good News. Truly, Jesus tells the Pharisees that the man's congenital visibility impairment was not because of sins incurred by him or his family. The person's blindness was allowed so that God's power might be revealed to others. That's enough for me and my family, too. If you'll excuse me, good day."

Normality Nouveau en Grace

A professor and long time friend/mentor I genuinely respect wrote to me on Facebook the other day. He wanted me to know that he'd been praying for me. I felt very honored to have received an email out of the blue like that. The message went on to explain why he'd been thinking of me because he was reading a self-help book discussing platitudes regarding the acceptance of, a "new normal." The idea of a new normal was originated by author Jill Briscoe in her book, *The New Normal*, published on September 16, 2005. She wrote this book to help grieving US Americans enlist strategies for comprehending that living the American life has been altered for most citizens due to 9/11. Dysfunctional suspicion, overarching confusion, roller coaster economics and uncontrollable weather patterns… these ideas applied to the macro society of the USA derive for all of us, this "new normal."

Since her authorship of this simple idea, a cacophony of psychologists and sociologists have chimed their interpretations across volumes of literary works. In my opinion, the USA has a populace that by and large craves wise originality. But its as though some choose to apply hermeneutical analysis to engage paradigms intended for a single purpose in other areas of life.

Raised to perceive differences between the areas of the mind-body continuum, I have a hard time accepting some idea of some "new normal." At least for the very hallmark of a brain injury to where the person I am inside remains hidden from social consciousness. It irritated me at first because yes, I should accept the reality of my new limitations - bad back, injured vocal chord, C-7 facial nerve damage, TBI, gold eye weight, constant eye-watering, short temper - but that which I am forced physiologically to allow others behold cannot begin to match who I am inside.

Does that mean that I should be content with lashing out verbally at friends and family, or in moments of pain, end up severing dear relationships and burning bridges? In my opinion, TBI is radically different from many handicaps, but I only perceive my reality through the personal lens of ethnography, so I can't speak for others. Nevertheless, I have decided that the turmoils, frustrations, pangs of sorrow, grief over lost hopes and dreams, loneliness, and sadness are not really anyone's business to judge. Perhaps thats why life-works are published only upon the death of authors and composers, because if you're alive, you have to argue and debate; something my personality-type is resigned to avoid.

Yet, at the same time, while the culture of disability is not anyone's business, the results of perceptions directed towards existing differences should be discussed more often in my opinion.

The harshest reality of some ideology procuring a new normalcy is that human beings operate in a perfect present tense. My identity and the motivation for that which I would do is unattainable. Accepting some new normal would entreat me to say goodbye to myself entirely. Despite so many good intentions of others, it is simply something I cannot do. Certainly, I will not.

Truly, survivors may manifest as fish-out-of-water, but they must be allowed the chance to continue in the directions they were heading at the moment of traumatic impact if at all possible. The importance of upholding personal identity is the key to every experiment studying social reintegration. Recreating personality is a horribly daunting procedure and takes great amounts of time, patience and effort, but this too, can be done.

It doesn't make a speck of difference who you are, I have never met my match in someone with boundaries except for girls that allow their mothers to speak for them. Many people like to say they have them, but they don't. What the masses have is control, and they confuse the two more often than not. For example, a conversation between two adults whose emotions aren't triggered, boundaries. Conversing with another adult basing your perceived viewpoint allowing triggered emotions... should be obvious, that's control.

The whole lot of human behavior is so fascinating because while we each yearn for something better than ourselves, we consistently belittle and naturally fight. That natural fighting is most likely the output of the evolutionary process. How else can an individual get rid of one who judges, but by making them feel utterly lost in a world of hardship.

I will always contest, that my God and I understand each other — that is not for anyone to debate, judge, or decide. The world's most spiritually elite guidance counselors might instruct a life of close fellowship to the Body, but what did they say to the Prophets? Anyone with a message of change is murdered or excluded from the nucleus of group thought. Why in heavens is this so?

If your survivor is annoying you because they are mourning their lost identity, it's okay to propose new ideas for them to possibly interact with others. It is so important for the vast number of us who survive severe brain trauma that people conceptualize the sadness due to TBI is not a mental issue. In every possible way, the morphology of a survivor's personality into one sharing acquired disability is substantial.

The carriage's roll, nay! my horses run;
How I think of you my dearest one!
Where are you now? Again, yet out of view.
Like my shadow, how I follow you!
Disappeared! Though, just in shade,
Now in the sun, don't ever fade.

— Fu Xuan From, *The Carriage's Roll*

CHAPTER 12

IT REALLY WAS A MIRACLE, WHAT HAPPENED WAS JUST THIS

In 1999, I received a prestigious vocal scholarship to begin college. As part of the fulfillment, I had been invited to promote the college in song at various supporting churches every few weeks. I distinctly remember unbuckling my seatbelt in the parking lot after ordering breakfast lying down in the middle backseat of the 15-passenger van. Me and my singing team, 'Anonymous,' were traveling that Saturday morning to our second performance venue at the First Christian Church in Fayetteville, Arkansas.

Growing up in Branson, I was very familiar with the route we would be taking on the highway through Springfield, and that's likely why I felt so comfortable to lie down. About six miles west of Springfield though, something popped. Feeling the start of fish-tailing, I sat up when our Alto in the passenger seat called my name. I noticed that Beth's hands were sprawled out, stiffly holding onto the dashboard, and I heard Daphne scream. "What's going on back here?," I said. Daphne said, "I'm so sorry, I don't know what happened!"

We were going about 65-75 miles an hour or so. And I think Beth told her to let off the break and at some point also let go of the steering wheel.

"Bryan, say a prayer!" Beth shouted out, half-turned.

I saw Daphne cup her right hand in the air, lifted up and she was calling out to God for help, but I have no memory of the actual accident that followed. I've reconstructed the story from my perspective with the help of others involved as these things were told to me. The OCC van wheeled into the median and then somersaulted five times and landed on its side. I had been ejected through a rear window during the second or third modulation and was laying consciously in pain surrounded by dying tall grass, my head pounding relentlessly and my right shoulder girdle unable to move.

When leaving Joplin, the temperature was still in the low 50s, and I think in the ditch it was still a bit damp and cool. It was mildly breezy with wind speeds recorded that day at around 18mph (*weather.com*). A woman from Kansas, I think her name was Amy, stopped to see what had happened. Going to the van, the young mother could hear girls crying and praying, seatbelted into the toppled van.

Holding on to the left driver's side tire, Amy navigated the undercarriage with her feet and leaned into the window. She asked, "Are you okay in here?" Daphne tried to help Amy balance herself, but as she lunged forward, she realized the seatbelt had cut deeply into the left side of her neck. She reached her hand out to Amy though and responded, "Hello! Thank you for stopping.

We lost a tire I think and I couldn't control the steering or brakes. I'm bleeding and the seat belt cut into my neck and Beth, are you okay?"

"I think so, my head really hurts, but our friend isn't responding. His name is Bryan. He was in the backseat and I think he got thrown out the window when the van was rolling."

"Okay girls," she said, "anyone else?"

"No we're just a trio," Daphne said.

Turning around, the Kansas mother started walking through the luggage and sound equipment, speakers, etc; but when she saw my body in the median, her eyes welled and she came to me quickly.

She knelt down and placed her hand on my forehead. After taking a refreshed breath, she spoke to me.

"Hi Bryan, I'm Amy. What happened?"

"I'm not sure, I think I fell out the window. My lower back hurts real bad. I can't move my arm; and my head is killing me."

"I have some training as a nurse; I'm not supposed to move you right now, but the Springfield ambulance is on its way, though. We're gonna get you to the hospital real soon, okay? Can I get you anything while we wait, are you thirsty?"

Squinting from the sun's rays in my face, "I'm so cold," I replied.

"It's gonna be okay, sweetheart. I'll be right back, I'm gonna get some water bottles and washcloths from my car for your friends."

"Alright, thank you."

She raced back to her car to retrieve her baby's blanket and some water bottles. As she began walking back to the van, a green truck pulled up along the median on the other side. The driver got out and came right to me before she could get back. The middle-aged male had black, scraggily hair, a mustache/beard, and wore worn blue jeans. My clothes were torn from the glass and I had minor scrapes and bruises, but I still was not bleeding externally. Before Amy had reached us, he said, "God needs to speak with you, son," in a low, assuring voice.

"I'm his servant, but I'm not dead. Just in a lot of pain," I said to him. He cradled my head with his large, rough hands and said,

"It's alright, but you're not bleeding and I need to move your head."

"Amy said I'm not supposed to move until the ambulance gets here."

"She sounds like a smart lady, I'm glad she was here to help you. On the count of three, okay."

"One,"

"But my shoulder is broken, man."

"Two,"

"Dude, I can't!"

"Three."

Amy said I let out a yell, and that's what made her turn away from the girls. Jake had turned my neck so precisely that I began bleeding profusely out my left ear. By the time Amy had returned, I was unconscious, and not breathing. As she got closer, she saw my face turned and blood gushing from my left ear, she grimaced like a mother bear and called out,

"Hey! You! Stop!" The man backed away.

"What's your name?"

"Jake," he said.

"Where did you come from?"

"I saw the van and wanted to help."

Amy knelt down and counted my pulse. "What have you done to his ear, he wasn't bleeding when I arrived on the scene."

"Same as you, ma'am just trying to help the boy."

"You do realize that moving an injured body at the scene of an accident is a crime, don't you? His right shoulder is broken! You could have killed him!"

"Yes ma'am, but he wasn't bleeding. Cranial pressure can kill a kid in a situation like this."

Shifting her gaze to his battered, green Chevy, she asked him, "And you," she took a quick second to swallow. "You, have medical training?"

"Yes, ma'am," he said as though it were as matter of fact as his degree.

"Let me give you a hand with that blanket." Bending down to sit by me, he opened his hands to receive the blanket.

Amy unfolded the blanket and wrapped it over my arms, while Jake mimicked her to cover my opposite side.

Amy's mind was racing with questions... who is this backwoods man? Why was he traveling away from town? Practically asking, she cried out in her mind, "Lord, please protect this boy, after being injured, this man tried to kill him!" The tears were falling slowly from her blank face.

Jake saw her lips moving as if to say, "Lord." At that moment, he reached out and grabbed her hand in a way that was reassuring. "Have you been praying for Bryan?" he asked.

She wiped the streams from her cheeks and answered, "Yes, since the moment I saw the van."

"I believe God makes things happen for a reason. I was not needing to come this way this morning. I'll stay here with Bryan, but I think you should go make sure the girls are okay; only just keep praying... don't stop."

More cars were beginning to stop themselves and see what was happening there on I-44. I'm sure not everyone that was on the road that day stopped, but I'm so thankful for those that did. Jake and Amy were trying to answer questions of people now standing around the accident site.

The ambulance arrived a moment or two later. Amy walked toward the EMT and introduced herself.

"Thank you for coming so quickly," she said. "The two girls are still trapped inside the van," she smiled with relief that the EMT had come.

Grabbing his medical bag, the point-person replied, "Alright, and the boy?"

"Yea." She pointed her slender arm and index finger, "He's over there in the tall grass."

"This way, guys," the head technician said, and two emergency nurses ran with him to my side. Unpacking the medical bag and assessing the situation, the EMT persons worked quickly, in harmony together.

The head technician leaned into the microphone affixed to his shirt while pressing the intercom button at his belt. "This is EMT Springfield 5-5-5 and we're needing to request the Life-Flight at this time."

The operator replied, "10-4, please confirm your location."

"Yes sir, we're about 12 miles west of the hospital. Patient is unconscious in-between farm roads 89 and 91 in the median of I-44."

"10-4, location determined. We're on our way, over and out."

"10-4, over and out." He then grabbed his clipboard and motioned for just Amy to come near. "Is this how you found him?"

Glancing briefly at Jack, she turned back towards the EMT. Flashing her medical badge nonchalantly, she whispered, "I didn't want to move anything... or anyone. But this man turned his head. He was still conscious when I arrived. I even spoke to him."

The EMT sighed, "That's good to know. How long would you estimate the boy went without oxygen?"

"Probably just over a minute or so, from the time his head was moved to the time your ambulance team arrived."

"Did you witness the accident?"

"No. The van completed its final roll as I began to brake."

"Can you describe what you saw after you'd stopped?"

"My first thought was that someone had died so I called my friend at the trauma center from my cell phone. I've never actually seen one of these collisions in real life before, but I went straight to the driver's side as the van was on its side. I heard two girls crying, and when I asked to help, they told me this boy, Bryan, had flown out the window."

"And that's when you brought him the blanket?"

"No sir, that's when I found him and spoke to him. He told me he was cold. I went to my car to grab burping cloths for the girls to stop their bleeding. While I stopped to pray quickly with the girls in the van, my back was still turned, but I heard Bryan scream. When I turned around, that's when I saw this man's hands on his head. I ran over and was a bit rude to this Jack or Jake guy, but I told him that he should stop trying to help. It was then I think that I noticed the blood streaming from his left ear."

The Main Technician motioned for Jake to join him and Amy off to the side of the tall grass. At this time, police had accumulated directing traffic to clear a landing area for the emergency helicopter, which would soon be landing. "Jake, part of my job requires interviewing eye-witnesses of any accidents I help with in Springfield's jurisdiction. Did you see the accident?"

"No sir."

"What made you stop?"

"I heard the boy."

"What do you mean, from your car?"

"I saw Amy helping the girls in the van and when I got out of my truck, I heard and saw the boy in the tall grass."

Amy interrupted, "He's lying, Bryan was not making any sounds until this man moved his head!"

The technician placed his hand on Amy's shoulder, "Okay now, just hold on a minute."

Jake just drew his lips together, "I heard you, too," he said softly with eyes of unwavering calm.

"Mr. Jake, now when you approached the boy, was his body as it is now?"

"Not quite, no."

The technician thought he would offer more of an answer, but without further hesitation, he opened his palm, "Can you explain?"

A systematic, firing rhythm of the Life Flight® was faintly heard in the distance.

"Yes, sir. When I approached the boy, he was talking softly and incoherently. I knelt down to encourage him and placing my hands carefully behind each ear, I turned his head sharply without damaging the bony structures. It was at that moment that blood began emanating from his left ear."

"Why would you do that?" The head technician asked.

"Respects, sir, but if he didn't begin bleeding, he could have died."

By this time, the helicopter was beginning to descend to the roadway. The head technician shouted, "I need you both of you to stay put and I'll be back with some contact forms after Bryan gets loaded on the helicopter."

Amy rejoined the girls still inside the van. She updated them on the situation, "Beth! Daphne!" She shouted over the helicopter. "Your friend Bryan is being Life-Flighted to Cox Hospital in Springfield. He went for about a minute without oxygen and he's unconscious. I'm right here, but we'll help you more when the helicopter leaves."

Inside the OCC van, the picture of peace could be heard as Beth and Daphne cried and prayed. Outside the van, however, the area looked reminiscent of a battle-zone in chaos. Police officers lined the roads, traffic was at a stand-still, a helicopter was on the interstate, a van was on its side in the median with just three wheels and everyone's attention seemed to follow the body bed being lifted into the helicopter. Not quite the showmanship performance of the year I'd been preparing for OCC's annual, "Living Christmas Tree," singing Sleigh Ride by Irving Berlin with my tap shoes; but it was the birth of a new performance that would be more integrative involving my mouth, sensory and postural functions much more than I could even have imagined had someone told me.

Once the helicopter was in the air, the chief technician organized the necessary signature forms in the ambulance glove compartment. Then walking briskly, he tugged on a police officer's jacket and asked her to take Jake into custody. The technician explained his preliminary findings above the fading roar of the chopper and the officer agreed. But something happened. Before the highway lanes had cleared, before the girls were removed from the van, before the helicopter's rhythmic cypher was even out of sight… Jake was gone. After speaking to Amy, they all were surprised to discover that in the midst of a dozen police officers, 7 nurses, unmovable lanes, an ambulance in the median, the OCC van on its side and several cop cars, the green Chevy® pickup had just… in a word… vanished. After interviewing drivers in their vehicles… no one on the roads could remember seeing a green truck. The Springfield police issued a bolo for the pickup truck that morning; but a whole twenty-three years later, its never been found.

It never hurts to keep looking for sunshine.

— Eeyore A.A. Milne

CHAPTER 13

MINE, A TBI

When I regained consciousness in the hospital, my working memory was not functioning, and would not fully begin working until the day I left the hospital almost three months later on December 24th. I could barely move and as to that which I've alluded earlier in this book, I was unable to speak. Not from loss of words, mind you, but unable to remind myself how to talk. This does not mean that I was unable to think, I was quite cognizant of describing my surroundings - at least to myself - but in every way I was beholden to an almost indescribable entanglement of injurious dysfunction.

According to the medical files accumulating during my interlude as a patient, I was in a comatose for nearly three weeks. At the beginning of my loss of consciousness in the median on Highway 65, I nearly died. During my first night in the hospital, I gained substantial pressure under the cranium and almost died a second time. As they prepared to insert a shunt, the pressure began to dissipate. Both times, I was substantially lucky. My parents identified my bruised and broken body that day and proceeded to call our relatives from Colorado, Nebraska, Wisconsin and Texas.

After projected outwardly of a non-opening side window of that 15- passenger van, I sustained multiple injuries that I will now describe in order, from my feet to the head. The injury most distal to my head included the lowest vertebrae of my back's lumbar region, where it joins with the sacrum of the pubic girdle. Moving proximally (towards the head) my right elbow incurred an array of frustrating effects.

During my bout in comatose, the physicians and nurses could not exercise my right arm. Because of broken bones in my shoulder girdle, my elbow joint froze due to the accumulation of a biological by-product produced under duress. Despite several surgeries to release my elbow, recruiting the strongest male nurses to bend my elbow, and countless hours of painful physical therapy, my elbow still does not completely bend or straighten a full 100%. My left vocal cord was partially paralyzed through this ordeal of trauma.

My first attempts at producing vocative sounds (nearly 3 months after waking from a coma) were made not from the vocal cords but from my right vocal cord vibrating with muscles in my throat. Crazy.

The left-side, C-7 facial nerve was stretched, bruised, and nearly cut in two by the bones surrounding my inner ear. The trauma in this location also affected my ability to hear 100% in my left ear, which was a huge problem for me during the first 5 years inside the TABLÆS.

Then to crown the entirety of the situation, my brain injury was, in a word, complex. Evaluating the overall unit of the skull, a total of 36% of those bones were either fractured or broken. The occipital bone was broken in half in addition to 8 fractures on the surface of the skull.

From a summary of my Physicians' reports, the records indicated parenchymal hemorrhage epidural & subdural hematoma's with perhaps the most compounding issue of brain shearing. A shear brain injury is typically severe when added to a brain injury because it's strikingly different when compared with "whiplash." People are fairly concerned with the issues of tightness to bodily areas after experiencing whiplash. Although, not everyone is commiserates with what transpires from a shear brain injury. It's whiplash to the brain multiplied by 100. In addition to propelling the body forwards and immediately backwards, as is customary with whiplash; the brain itself shakes, gravitates, and violently rotates inside the skull, which is described by the term "shearing."

"I find no room containing sorrow," regretful, reason wept. Yet with the bud, a new tomorrow, achieve, forgive, and accept.

— Bryan Sisson

CHAPTER 14

COMPLICATED DRAMA

I fear you may grow weary of shining your beacon, or remaining truly focused on that which you believe to be your life's purpose post-trauma. People will constantly argue with you because they assume 1) you're on pain killers or 2) they actually think they can diagnose the effects of your injury better than countless doctors or anyone else trained on the subject of TBI. I know for me, my life would be *countless* moments of drama if I allowed people to get the better of me. I don't need their approval, nor do I need their narrow lens of depression to super-impose onto the happiness I live. But that's way easier said than done.

Looking back over my own time on the TABIÆS, I will account for a few specific situations where instead of just standing resolute and posing my argument, something I cannot do post-trauma, I am funneled towards a harder path - remaining silent and walking away. Among the top things that acquired difference has taught me to be content with is a) swallowing my pride, b) life is what you make it, and although cliché, c) money buys little more than loneliness. Rephrasing Zondervan's *Word on the Street*, "When the people of a village, or family, or friends refuse to accept your message, your identity, your handicap, turn on your heels and shake their dust from your feet, get rid of their negativity, and go on trusting that the Lord, that life, that the universe will continue to provide for your interests: bad or good, rich or poor."

Very often, people want to continue displaying a sort of herd mentality, or group mode where everything is labeled mentality and individuate from the norm, they become a threat to the group's idea of survival. During graduate school, I experienced the first of these complicated drama sequences from which I was forced to just walk away, something I would never have done pre-trauma.

Nonetheless, 7 years into the TABLÆS, I had been granted permission to conduct my very first ethnographic program evaluation with the Crow Creek Sioux Tribe Reservation youth group, *Peers Helping Peers*. Because of their sovereign nation agreement with our USA, they asked me to not publish my practicum and thesis or to discuss my findings outside the setting of the University of North Texas. Of course I agreed, because in many ways the Tribal Council had given me my Native calling as a grown man, as a member of society. But when my family pushed me to talk with family friends of what happened during my stay on Indian land and I refused, you can only imagine the kind of backlash I encountered from all sides.

As a survivor - well, as an anthropologist - placing blame on specific individuals is not entirely fair. This is why qualifying attitudes or events as good or bad during the story does little more than manifest angst in those who buy-in to certain perspectives. The job of the anthropologist is to present an event or story as unbiasedly as possible so that the individual reader can judge for themselves from the observance of all the facts.

My contact on the reservation pulled away shortly after this due to his job and the tireless responsibilities given him by the Tribal Council; and for what seemed like the first time in my life as an adult, I was left to defend my stance on my own. Upholding the contract I had created and signed with the Internal-Review-Board at North Texas, I muttered, sputtered, and had long gaps between sentence fragments. Some pointed to the fact that I had looked to the left, others commented on the fact that I had touched my nose several times, others pointed to the fact that because of where they were in relation to me I looked like i was terrified, maybe even angry!

I will share with you that referring to something as easy as saying, "Oh, well I can't discuss that because of my agreement with the IRB at UNT;" was ridiculously unavailable to me at this point on my TABLÆS. During graduate school I thought partly that speaking so many words to explain simple concepts was strictly because of my increase in conceptually academic wisdom. The reality as I look back to this time period is actually a clinically based symptom relative to my recovery on the TABLÆS.

In line with my personal trajectory, I have found that the medical community's identification of head injury symptoms is more likely to be possible if properly organized qualitative experiential knowledge. Verbosity initiates a unique inability to speak in as few words as possible to communicate an idea or request. To me the interesting thing about the use of a survivor in verbosity is not in the number of words used but in the type of words used. While still expressing the complex and theoretical framework on TBLÆS as a survivor, I believe I used an overwhelming supply of words from junior high and/or high school. Even when I took the GRE, my verbal score was pretty low; so thank goodness for dictionaries.

How can the survivor defend natural body movements when trauma causes them to jump and jive? How can survivors defend the way others assume survivor's intent because if the left C-7 facial nerve is off? How can awkwardness be removed from a situation if agitated silence persists between words? How!? The problem is this, no-one thinks to consider that the misgivings and awkwardness in your face could have causes other than your emotions. You find out much later that these feelings and individual premonitions contributed to the efficacy of your damaged defense. And usually you find out too late, when the relationship has been too greatly severed for any hope or idea of repair. My time on the Reservation was the first secret I ever kept from my family, maybe this is bad since I was already 24 years old, and maybe it was good, but thats not for me to decide.

What happened from here is that some people thought I had maliciously assisted suicide-attempts by youth on the Reservation secretly. The thought makes me sick, and nothing could be more false! *YUCK!* I spent the summer in South Dakota saving lives, not hurting them. Remember from chapter 6 about the inability for the brain to communicate under high amounts of projected stress. Never, never, ever, speak down to your traumatized individual when your personal perceptions are unwarranted or exaggerated. And if you are traumatized, remember to try not to dwell too long attempting to identify what might have made a social situation different or better.

Dwell... well, swell! It's a funny sounding word in all honesty, but duh- well-ing on a subject from personal history can really accomplish next to nothing for an individual. An old friend once said to me, "You dwell on past encounters so much that you end up sustaining the social problem instead of learning to deal with it."

It caught me so off guard that I got a pit in my stomach. This was the moment on my personal ethnography when I comprehended that it's okay to not always speak everything you know to be true. I bit my tongue every time he said that, because I knew it was caused by my brain injury... it was perseveration. I don't know your survivor or the deficits sustained with their trajectories, but as per my experience, it takes a sufficient quota in years to match thoughts, words, actions, etc with their appropriate, physical age.

At my worst memorable moment in life (two months or so after waking from comæd-slumber) I still remember the first few words I spoke when asked what I'd like to do with my life's purpose. I heard the answer. Growing up in a highly conservative home where patriarchal dominance was the lead, I was taught never to listen to evil thoughts, but always remain true and speak for myself. I certainly don't know everything, but in my opinion all the tools used towards enculturation of survivors will unfold a second-time commiserate with the order of childhood as the brain floods with unconscious memories. Looking back on that event in the hospital, I'd say I was about on the level of a kindergartner when I spoke the answer I heard in my head.

Some scientists believe that every time your brain creates a new memory, a new "connection" or pathway is forged between neurons in the brain. I suppose that the later in life trauma is introduced, the subsequent steps towards complete recovery might very well be that much more difficult. Although, with the amount of technological and medical increase concerning knowledge about the human brain, we humans are practically light years ahead of where it was only 100 years ago. But we're still not quite there yet.

When we think of great mystery religious wisdoms, many people's souls are stirred when we say or read the conclusion that "everything will be to you as it was before." Clichés, idioms, wise sayings, etc. that have little place within the context of adulthood, can at times have prominent affects on others when actively discussed by survivors afflicted by disability. I'm definitely not saying that a brain injury provides some golden ticket for living life in a fairy tale or even a sort of insidious cake-walk for that matter! At the same time, I'm just attempting conveyance of realities inherent to life on the TABIÆS. For reasons I will share, some sort of journaling process will be integral to the grounding of a survivor's psyche.

Re-learning to judge oneself and evaluating personal progress realistically might cause bewildering amounts of stress for the survivor. Especially during the first few years following the traumatic experience, a survivor will likely not possess the wherewithal to compare themselves to their shadow-selves. Be patient and encouraging, because the profound meaning of their survival personality post-trauma will manifest at the appropriate time. It may present more quickly for some than others, but the realization is appropriate only by the survivors themselves. Parents and guardians cannot tell their survivors of perceived difference acquisition, they must learn their new identities in ways both natural and individually, but never rushed.

Appropriate and lasting recovery takes time using baby steps and watching grass grow. To pose differently, the objective reality of a new normal at this point should be freely understood and accepted. However, survivor's subjective analyses of their new acquired personalities absolutely entail a foundation of laying to rest the shadow-self. Only when the shadow personality's hopes and dreams have been adequately mourned and all avenues of trial-and-error for achieving said goals have been explored and further exhausted can the new identity emerge. This transfiguration in personality accepts the acquired differences and allows understanding changes created in relationships. The transfigured personality further entails a hidden ability towards self-control and any necessary modifications that can help a survivor navigate the social sphere with success.

Identifying age-appropriate perception. When a parent/caregiver teaches a child that something is age-appropriate or not condoned in a particular setting, they have a few tools in their educational/behavioral tool-belt. Perceived authority, size, strength, responsibility, family history, love, self-control. These constructs play a significant role in building the respect our elders deserve. Well, we perceive those continuums until hormones begin producing. That's usually when human beings start thinking of reproductive behaviors.

Its my opinion that while on the TABLÆS, the ideology of a sexual nature becomes almost primal. There's a reason that either God or nature's heuristics caused our bodies to produce hormones in our teens. Picture a toddler that loves to run naked, always takes his clothes off at the grocery store and surprises Grandma in the frozen-foods section... its innocent behavior. Picture that same child in her/is twenties a few years post-trauma... s/he gets naked whenever, wherever s/he can, takes her/is clothes off in public and exhibits unsavory social behavior towards others to whom s/he is attracted... its difficult to judge, because in my mind, it's different.

Do you remember when as a young teen, even the slightest amount of skin exposed could stay with you for hours? Or for young girls that might feel so safe, respected and loved that they would do anything for their boyfriend? Its true that human beings are afflicted (or blessed) by an animalistic nature that makes our bodies crave mating behaviors. But its also true that we are either blessed with (or afflicted by) consciousness. Perhaps Chinese philosophy establishes truth in the Yin & Yang, but our Western culture takes it to a whole other level by insisting that its archaic to mate for life, but secular to "have fun".

In a society that won't judge you for living your life, there are countless cultures that will. Remember when I said, "If you want to find mistakes in your survivor, they will be abundant?" During recovery on the TABLÆS, the idea of "listening to one's body," becomes so engrained to the survivor's existence. Medical professionals provide stringent biological education without the implementation of social rules/customs, etc. as if social functioning is for recovering adults to relearn among their families and friends.

Counselors and various medical professionals comprehend that the survivor is most likely experiencing a different personality; but my experience and that of my family is that there is next to little in place for the sociocultural readaptation during time spent on the TABLÆS. PTSD in our service men and women is manifesting because its difficult if not impossible to place limitations on oneself once the cat of destructive behaviors is essentially "out of the bag". Its difficult for the families, I have witnessed, but the return to personality must be shaped outside the home in my opinion. Because of this reality, a magnanimous amount of mistakes will occur. The act of finding oneself is difficult enough the first time. Try adding a brain injury the second time and confusion persists.

As I've tried to show in this book, recovery from severe closed-head injury is not portrayed correctly by media, on various self-help websites, and even in countless literatures that address the cause-and-effect scenarios of sport concussions and mild TBIs. The farther away the survivor is removed from his age-line, the longer, I believe, s/he will spend on the TABLÆS.

I have a professional, Facebook® relationship with a lawyer in Massachusetts who helped me rationalize a lawsuit against a religiously-based insurance company in 2002. I felt so lost when I figured out the University I was attending had only wanted to pay enough to unplug the life- support machine. I thought they loved my singing voice and wanted me to keep singing, but how could I sing if I couldn't pay my way to get better? By the end of 1999, only 3 months after my accident mind you, my college "family" had moved on without regards to the injury I sustained. They had already forgotten about me before I had even remembered who I was. As I was saying these things, Michael interrupted me, "Its not that they forgot you, but how can they move forward if they're focused on helping someone from the past?"

When moving to Dallas in 2009, I began attending a small church on the way to Ft. Worth along I-30. I created strong friendships with those in the congregation, and finally felt like I had friends who were empathetic to my life. I told Kurt how the church loved to hear me sing, and how by merely being polite, the aggressive preacher's wife touched me inappropriately at worship rehearsals. I had signed up to help the mission trip to Guatemala one year prior, and explained how months later after the trip, the preacher put me blankly on the spot; asking questions while on stage during services, like, "so you've accepted that God healed you?"

"You're over it now! Praise God!"

Did God really ask Mary to just get over those birthing pains? I suppose some think that the Good Lord beseeched the wandering Jews to just forget about the sadness caused by desert hunger and thirst? Perhaps others even think that the Allah asked the Islamic Prophet to go through life penniless. My goodness, of all the distractions that we have on earth, we have got to learn to say, "If you don't judge me, I won't judge you."

When I was growing up and earning my stars in the Anita Bryant Company, Anita often sat in the back of the theater to observe our progress. Once, I remember my parents were with a few others of youth in our group that were sitting with Anita and a few other producers/ choreographers. One afternoon rehearsal, she took me aside to remind me, "Bryan, you and I both have booming voices, and no one questions your talent, but singing in a group means that you must listen for the group sound from the very softest singer." Then when the accident took my voice, the one thing I was best at, my identity became lost and confused.

In many ways, the loss of my identifiable talent is indeed reminiscent of a sports player or figure skater acquiring physiological differences from some sustained injury. The exclusiveness of head trauma is more complicated than first meets the eye. Yes, professionals are correct in highlighting the similarities between recovery trajectories. Additionally, counselors must adjust their defining of the critical likelihood that awareness of the survivor's shadow-self is important for attaining the age line on my TABLÆS.

People never give me the kind of overwhelming, standing ovations they did prior to acquiring my difference. They almost never remark on my singing as humans did before. Some have said that the cause is due to my age, because adults don't usually respond to talents in peers in the same way they would if it were exhibited by a teenager. At the same time, I don't want to project animosity onto my situation; but realistically, I ponder to what degree my C-7 facial nerve injury plays into people's perception of my ability to perform or be an enjoyable soloist.

Does that mean that I'm supposed to just "accept" this idea of "new normal" to where others never see me as the person I am? I am a performer, its how my mind operates, but its not how my body is able to produce. Does this mean I'm depressed? NO! Does it mean I'm any less than the man I always want to be? NO! Does it mean I'm different from what I might have been? Absolutely. But I will not allow myself to scour among lost hopes forever.

Finding your purpose post-TBI is going to be difficult. Locating a calling and developing passion for something new may never present itself in the ways you always remembered. People will give you different looks that won't register in your psyche; but you'll realize those glances are identical to those you've seen given to others subconsciously pre-TBI. Accepting yourself and being proud of your accomplishments post-TBI may take work to actually feel good about those things in which you've succeeded. Understanding that your body may do things you cannot control post-TBI may be for you a daily struggle. But this is because the mind has forgotten rules of social intercourse, i.e. for some of us, our natural explicit memory is turned off now. It may be hard to keep up with conversations in noisy areas and it will be very easy for you to be misunderstood.

For most of my friends, crazy and loud, reverberating bass dance music is invigorating and provides a pep in their step. Often when some people see an individual with a TBI, they will judge the person as somehow forlorn and depressed... perhaps even out of place. But as I've admonished before, a TBI does not equal depression or non-comfort with oneself! The loud pounding bass actually causes pain in the brains of some trauma-survivors. It"s difficult to not feel as though you're always watching a motion-picture screen in some theater instead of actively living in the present.

"Like the lotus flower,
life is unfolding just as it should."

—Buddha

CHAPTER 15

PROJECTION VS. DISCRETION

Post-injury and several years into recovery, there will come a point to which communication becomes unreliable and confusing. The realm of understanding is only as deep as one's ability to comprehend. In other words, the paradigm of society is only as far reaching as one's cultural development permits. One cannot include varying levels of comprehension when the brain is unable to transmit messages successfully syncretic ally from various portions of the brain with personal history, present experience and future goals.

Encouragement is a vital necessity along the TABIÆS. But make certain your encouraging words are free of internal projections. In my own academic history, some might perceive my scholarly choices as mistakes. Conversely though, I believe that everything in a person's life is meant to happen. However, by itself, trajectories do not define those with acquired differences. The active discipline of managing personal experience develops and sustains personal spirit. When reflecting on the survivors' "lotus flower" — that is, how they navigate through life's sociocultural consciousness — we not only see their reality, but begin to understand the character of acquired difference.

The truth of that "lotus flower" can frustrate the survivor though. During recovery, internal frustrations towards everything abound. Its difficult, but the only means of achieving success is finding open ways of communication. When you feel slighted, get hurt feelings, feel like you can't live life, etc. step back and be silent. Draw a few deep breaths to calm your body and repeat the peribology of the Buddha's statement.

You're okay because life is operating... the lotus flower unfolds. Of course, you may never have experienced life quite like what happens in the aftermath of a brain injury; but everything — social mistakes, weird sentence structures, verbosity, wrong word-choice, misbalancing of finances, societal frustrations, inward emotions, etc. — (all of it) will work out in the end to exactly what is meant to be. Living life as a survivor takes skill, and if you really can't accept the new you, please take initiative in seeking counseling, art or physical therapy until you're able to find new hobbies. Don't just wait for the newness to descend. It will come to you, I promise; but the TABLÆS is a process. Some might say trust the universe, follow the goddess or even have faith! The concrete reality though for any and every survivor is that our trust resides in time made manifest through experience.

Think again about the TABLÆS. Perhaps not all will experience the magnitude of my own trajectory; and with your reading of my ethnography, I hope less and less will struggle with the anguish from reflection over their acquired difficulties. At some point, the survivor is going to retaliate against the idea of disability and handicap. It's inevitable and must almost always be permitted. In my opinion, the impetus for this unique frustration is constructed by the survivor's intercourse with society. The rudeness encountered by strangers and friends is inversely proportional to the mistaken cruelty shown, if at all, by their cultural representative family-of-chance. In other words, the lateral violence experienced pre-trauma will create the hierarchical self-displayed ideological violence.

Returning to a state of normalcy, regaining 100% consciousness of a survivor's pre-trauma personality, may be pretty much unattainable. Of course this is dependent on where the brain was injured, socioeconomic status and various characteristics that have been discussed in this book. As the survivor adapts to her/is new sequelae, some bouts of depression can at times develop. Even when aspects may be viewed by others as attributes better than the survivor exhibited pre-trauma, that unequivocal realization that the real you, your shadow-self, is no longer seen by those with whom the survivor interacts.

It must be understood by the non-traumatized that survivors will experience profound emptiness in a type of shell body that conceals the individual. In the first two years on the TABLÆS, and in many cases much longer than this, survivors attempt to re-engage with their culture and/or society commiserate with the skills and talents of their shadow-selves. Not all, but some survivors may experience a kind of hollowing when sociocultural perceptions of the transfiguring persona meet with different responses than those experienced by their shadows pre-trauma.

Not shadows in the sense that the individuals are not confident; but certainly in the guise of being rejection by people you're accustomed to being friends with. Some say that this is the "new normal". Others have attempted to tailor emotional healing strategies to help the survivor cope. The basis of why these methods don't work rests in the human mind-body of a survivor, we must contextually observe the mind-body continuum from the perspective of the body conceived in Ancient Egypt.

Ancient Egyptians believed that the human persona was divided 2 or 3 times more than the present, Western conception. They also held that the heart was the seat of consciousness and the gray stuff in the head was just present for some reason. Obviously, they were operating on a more primitive scale, but there is a construct that helps to explain the thought process of every survivor. The construct that should be added to Brain Injury Awareness is that of the shadow. Indeed there is much to be said of the ancient use of religion inside government and vice versa. However, a person's hope for what could/should/would have been was tied into the conceptualization of her/is shadow, something I earlier identified as the shadow-self.

As for survivors, the more distance acquired from the moment of trauma, they become increasingly aware of the looming shadow of whom they were, their unique social patterns, behaviorisms, and abilities that made them unique. Not always, but in many cases, talents, abilities and behaviors exhibited pre-trauma become lost. When trying to "act like s/he used to, the whole episode or exchange is bewilderingly tiring to the survivor. The brain's unique method of operation is actually what is injured. Enculturation by the parents or guardians of origin is wiped clean like a chalkboard during recess.

Individuals who knew survivor(s) pre-trauma can become frustrated with the survivor during recovery for the same reason that adults grow increasingly annoyed with little children. It should be paramount for every care-giver who understood the survivor pre-trauma to always be ready for engaging in conversation about her/is shadow. While the brain is re-mapping, identifying differences, similarities, new ideas on the pathway of life, the non-traumatized should listen to the survivor based on how they perceive themselves.

In graduate school, my professor-mentor surprised me on several occasions. She spoke about personal characteristic that she observed in me that I always felt I had excelled in, but had never heard anyone speak of it. Towards the fulfillment of my practicum and thesis, I was seated opposite the window. As she spoke of a few mistakes present in my paper, she noticed that my mind was wandering because my eyes were gazing just over the top of her head and into the trees.

She turned from her computer screen and looked me squarely in the eyes. "But Bryan," she said with a generous smile, "your ability to ponder emotional characteristics in others is quite fascinating." I do not mean to articulate that I am always correct or that I exhibit perfect behavior in all circumstances; it just so happened that I was in the right above board in my analysis of the suicidal conundrum at Crow Creek Sioux Tribe Reservation.

Its so important that loved ones acknowledge the survivor's shadow. Don't be pushy or overbearing, but help the recovering survivor rediscover themselves. Caregivers will not be able to do this using methods that may have worked when the survivor exhibited the same age characteristics as a child. This is because the survivor's brain has experienced a foundational paradigm shift, caused by the shearing, retrograde amnesia and to some extent the working memory. If you see something that is identical to what the survivor said, performed, or kinetically communicated pre-trauma; don't take that for granted. Voice the commonality to your survivor(s). Its possible they won't understand the movement or speech pattern as something they did, but even these subtle reminders allow the survivor to conceptualize internally that although they feel different, their shadow is observable and present.

Do what you can to keep the survivor from seeing you cry over lost hopes and dreams. Manifesting Severe TBIs is quite heartbreaking; but so much more when it involves someone you love or even yourself. Because emotional output is regulated by peripheral areas of the brain's frontal lobe, the realm of experiential feelings through body behavior, facial expressions, tears and articulating these emotions correctly becomes a con-fuddled mass of consistent confusion for survivors.

In many cases, the realm of communication will be dauntless for your injured survivor. As they formulate words and now have trouble connecting phrases, it's possible they will develop symptoms of anger and harshness that are unfamiliar to your history of knowing that person. Even when your injured person communicates emotions that are unfamiliar to you, I admonish you to talk about these ideas with your survivor(s).

Imperatively, never judge a survivor's thoughts as fully developed essays on a given subject; but in every case, discuss what your injured said by asking multiple open-ended questions. Perhaps, your injured person will not even have answers readily available, because throughout the rest of his/her life, the brain must be seen as though in a constant state of rejuvenation. The survivor should not be esteemed as childish, immature or even in certain situations, as stupid. Even though the learned intelligence.

The toughest times in my life post-TBI have descended upon me not because of the injury itself, but because some close to me decided beyond-the-shadows-of-doubt that because x-number of years since inducing TBI, recovery ought to have been attained. Family members, long-life friends, professors, colleagues, co-workers — no survivor — is spared from believing rumors that haunt this unseen injury. The many colors of attitudes socially projected onto this injury are countless.

The gaps in communication arising from the injury are surprising and repetitively unique. In normal non-TBI individuals, these gaps accompanied by side-glances, random eye twitches, and nose coverings are sure all-tell signs that such a person is lying or making up stories. For your TBI-injured however, do not fall susceptible to unfair diagnoses of the TBI individuals. During the brain's re-mapping cycles, any number of body movements or time-filling actions may occur during the 2-5 second gaps between words and phrases. If you have resolve to find mistakes in your survivor, you will find them.

Be it ever so severe should anyone determine that this writing unveils a blanket of dismissal for any wrongs done by someone with TBI. I am not saying that TBI creates some safe-haven for a wrong-doer. I am saying that mistreatment of the TBI-injured is wrong. The unseen handicap — this invisible injury — is defenseless. You'll remember in chapter 6, I told you about my counseling mentor, who said, "I can prepare you to ward off the stupid things people say and do." I will tell you that the ways in which people make of fun of you will be different, and this simple fact has the power, better or worse, to change your whole life.

It's true that the emotional and character output will be remarkably different from that which existed "pre-trauma." Countless self-help books will tell you that mourning for what's been lost is a necessary stage in the grieving process, and that the present is somehow now the normal, a point of personal acceptance, or revelation. I remember how irritated I would become bouncing back and forth between public and private colleges.

The religious students at Dallas Christian College would tell me, "Its okay to accept that you're life is different from what you thought it would be, thats the Holy Spirit's guidance." Their hearts are to be blessed, because they never knew I would later cry in my dorm room on the phone, "I thought I had consciously allowed the accident swap my choices to accept my handicapped nature." And then I would ultimately transfer to the University of North Texas and I often had an easier time because I chose the trauma's reality to define conceivable goals. I was still dissatisfied though, and I remember thinking to myself, "How can this be all there is to life? Surely there is something more."

Even though brain injury survivors won't always return to a level of normalcy, we all share this search for a life's purpose during the post-trauma phase. From the moment of regaining consciousness, there is a period of consistent successes, while the remapping of the brain achieves consistent and measurable goals aimed towards survival. Every time we do something good, reciprocal excitement exudes from the medical staff, family and friends.

It's taken awhile for me to realize this, so please don't be offended or expect your loved one to arrive at this thought too quickly. I postulate that brain injured people have difficulty discovering their life's purpose because the impetus for life's goals unconsciously shifts internally towards the act of instinctual survival. From the moment we emerge onto the social plateau, our social "game" is tainted because we survived.

The reason I think this exists is because subconsciously we're looking for a style of social affirmation which persisted during the unconsciousness of our second birth provided by the medical staff in our everyday lives. Society thinks in terms of etiquette, TBI cultures in terms of survival. The world of human behavior subconsciously adheres to a host of unwritten cues and verbal phenomena that cannot be retaught during the on-site, hospital recovery phase. Individuals adapting to redefined and/or new lives can only learn through the unbearable successions of trial and error within their realized age-equivalence spectrum.

In the wake of post trauma, you're going to find disquiet and unrest at each stage of development and/or reconnection. You'll fight this unending struggle the rest of your life. Whether or not you'll want to choose a familial, cultural, societal or globalized lens to project your personal history. Still, some may be so adaptable to their new personalities that they will allow the memories of themselves pre-trauma to be forgotten. I contend such religiously motivated self-help books and I challenge modern thought with the following supposition. The memory of anyone's trauma is culturally significant, but society cannot realize what they missed in forgetting you or your loved one.

That's the truth! If there is a realization that your past was the best part of you, start small. What I mean to say is be kind to yourself. In redefining your life's goals and incorporating a history of new talents is going to take time. I believe you can achieve great things as a survivor. It's just that the path to new discovery may be littered with unforeseen challenges. Don't get ahead of yourself and don't listen to anyone that is not your doctor! Climbing out of the TABLÆS will require every ounce of strength, you can muster, but the non- traumatized will likely perceive that you're simply working through some phase… "growing up". It's natural for many people to miss the social stature they had achieved pre-trauma, but it's unnatural to place limitations on yourself post-trauma. And therein lies a commonality between most survivors.

The Brain
The brain is wider than the sky,
For, put them side by side,
The one the other will include
With ease, and you beside.
The brain is deeper than the sea,
For, hold them, blue to blue,
The one the other will absorb,
As sponges, buckets do.
The brain is just the weight of God,
For, lift them, pound for pound,
And they will differ, if they do,
As syllable from sound.

—Emily Dickinson

CHAPTER 16

RECOVERING BRAIN

Perhaps you've read this book and decided that the writer is "off his knocker," or just depressed because he got a brain injury. Maybe you've read this book, and share in the cause to afford this writing as a plea towards fairness. Others might say that I'm just trying to engage and/or encourage blame and social drama. Regardless your view of my book, I'd like you to exhibit boundaries as I state my heart.

Life with acquired disability is, well… crabbed, to speak frankly. While I remember encouraging friends in high school that had visible handicaps, I never imagined that I should come to be counted among our number. Of course, I had been shocked by the stories of Olympians unable to perform at the last minute, but something like that wouldn't actually happen to anyone I knew, right? most certainly never to me, surely!… it couldn't!

My explicit memories of learned behaviors and social cues involving a filter of appropriation were hidden from my working memory. To this day, in fact, in many cases of anger, frustration and peer-pressure or needing to prove my stance on some given subject, the preknowledge of "going through the fire" is just not readily available. Knowing personal experience from similar social situations to help me rephrase my answers has not been immediately available while working at keeping up with conversation. The ability to give an unscripted account of my life set to a given context was additionally, but simply, not all there. For this reason, human behavior causes many to assume that I'm lying, exaggerating or presenting subconscious evidence of being raised in a dysfunctional home. Such ideas, however, are projected onto me regardless of any concrete proof or authentic awareness to my reality.

A social barrier should not be viewed as a more difficult consideration than a physical barrier. Altruistically, how much research and attention has been given to emotional barriers to people suffering from emotional trauma to achieve better functioning in society? When we consider everyone who experiences neurological disorders, TBI only represents a very small percentage.

The truth of the matter here is that I think our culture within the United States is expected to engulf, eradicate, and/or transform material qualities into attractive perfection. Of course, I don't believe this book will affect modifications to the way survivors interact with humans in the head injury paradigm. It is my sincere intention to help soften the painful shock you may potentially experience when the survivor's personality is in a position to change. Ultimately, accepting this pervasive idea of being tied by an acquired disability is what it means for your survivor and your family.

I want to reiterate that disabilities are not caused by evil or evil forces. Humanity has shown parts of time and space where persons with disabilities were respected and in some cases even worshipped. For some Native American cultures, such as the ancient Egyptians, disabilities and physical limitations were often observed because individuals with these unique traits were somehow closer to achieving godly enlightenment. I propose that it was not necessarily or never has been that survivors are closer to God, spirits, or privileged knowledge. The truth is that survivorship has the patience to wait for the appropriate time.

The secret of their iconic existences perhaps lay in their culture's desire to see each of them as a whole being, not a half-hearted or humorously provocative creature on the fringe. Consequently, the recovery paradigm alongside TABIÆS allows awareness of symptoms arising from direct brain injury and the rewiring process continues. Survivors do not always reveal some physical representation of certain emotional states. People with acquired disabilities have a more authentic ability to see the bigger picture, but only when the twenty years of recovery are completed.

I have a dear friend who is handicapped also due to a brain injury, although hers was an internal-closed-head injury caused by chemical imbalances in the brain. On the phone, my friend asked me, "Why do I have so much trouble just letting a question go? When I ask and ask and ask, I undoubtedly make others frustrated and they then tend to judge me as being weird, when all I'm trying to do is arrive at the underlying reason for why the group is talking about change." I know it may seem like this story is out of place, but so is the way with understanding brain injuries... confusing. Hold on though, reason will surface, just keep reading.

Through our 30-minute conversation, I tried to help her see that boundaries help us rationalize questions we have as either necessary or not. In many cases, questions survivors have - especially during the first 10 years along the TABLÆS - are truly none of our business to ask. Stepping back to look at the bigger picture, though, even non-survivors may ask this question. Why do brain injury survivors have such a propensity to ask questions of seemingly common sense answers? The answer in my opinion is that for survivors, where retrograde amnesia was introduced, the brain's ability to conjure working knowledge of past experience, while reframing it contextually, is unavailable to the survivor while on the TABLÆS.

My TBI and overall personality, education, etc. has helped me tremendously. Although, I have a distinct advantage here, because I'm post the 15-year recovery phase. Introducing that a chemically caused brain injury is not comparable to a closed head brain injury is important. At the same time though, the diverse affects of brain injury on the human psyche are similar.

My friend, Sally, suffered from some kind of exposure to liquid chemicals when she was a child. She is now in her early forties and functions very well. However, her symptoms have not changed in the course of five years that I've known her, while mine have improved. The sustained confusion troubling individuals with TBI is quite prevalent, in my opinion, in the first few years of recovery. Following detailed instructions, conceiving road directions, recipes and cooking successfully - just a few quandaries that should be very simple for even 3rd graders, will in fact present difficulties for survivors during the first few years of recovery.

Not all, but many of us, manifest social confusion that appears to be not just immature, but identified by others as stupid behaviors. The reality is this though, survivors are far from stupid. We just can be somewhat susceptible to social manipulation by persons in our sphere of consciousness, particularly during the five-twenty years following the moment of regained consciousness.

During the writing of this final chapter (December 2013), I was made aware of some inconsistencies on a website from a Facebook friend of mine researching the sociology of TBI in the Dakotas. She shared with me her bewilderment at the audacious claims provided on a factsheet of emotional problems following a Traumatic Brain Injury. I'd like to admonish the organization to provide more of a holistic lens when disseminating information concerning struggles exhibited by certain survivors. These are my personal reflections after purveying the webpage. I've had acquaintances, friends and one or two people in my own extended family perceive me in the way this site describes, and it made me laugh. However, when I asked how my friend came across the page, I grew increasingly upset.

An acquaintance of mine, who is a brilliant researcher in the Dakotas, helped me understand the Indian Health Service (IHS) when I was working on my graduate degree. We've remained in touch and occasionally exchanged ideas via Facebook®. When she found out I was writing this book, she told me how certain school systems were using a website to educate their students on some of the adverse side effects on emotions experienced by survivors following blunt traumas. The social worker shared with my friend how she found this "perfect explanation" on the internet... she had Googled, "Why are TBI folks so frustrating?" Needless to say, I was baffled, but because I can count a handful of people who have asked me that very question and likely used this site to "understand me better."

First of all, the organization claiming to foster a coherent understanding of TBI survivors describes us as being in a one-lump category, saying that, "most emotional problems will clear up after a few months." Secondly, the organization basically projects the emotional behaviors of survivors in terms reminiscent of the us and other. Shockingly similar to the highlights through which Malinowski described the peoples of the Trobriand Islands!

Not wanting to belabor the point, the organization to which I'm alluding goes so far to state that if you, yourself, as a TBI survivor experience frustrations in a given social setting, you should consult a medical doctor and possibly sign-up for anger management training. At first, I was mildly appalled by this vaguely academic approach to solving emotional outbursts exhibited by survivors. But it seems rather faux pas to me that anyone would articulate that 100% of social difficulties be attributed to the individual displaying brain trauma.

Ralph Waldo Emerson's perspective on social agility is good advice for all of us: "Adopt the pace of nature - her secret is patience." To individuals not affected by brain injury, logical reasoning implies that if you don't experience social awkwardness except when you're in the presence of a survivor, the awkward attitudes must surely be the fault of the survivor. Sometimes people seek to host a kind of intervention utilizing information acquired from the internet. The context is sincere, but the attitudes and perceptions might be slightly misguided.

Indeed, I don't believe any survivor would deny the fact that at times we manifest emotional lability. But to what degree this should be attributed to survivors themselves is the purpose of my book. Many survivors experience a unique symptom indicative of typical brain injuries called aphemia.

Invention, it must be humbly admitted,
does not consist in creating out of a void, but out of chaos.

— Mary Shelly

CHAPTER 17

THE TABIÆS

On the road of recovery, it is my belief, survivors approach recovery through ascension. Some might phrase this as climbing out of a pit entrenched in despair. Caretakers and loved ones of the surviving, however, realize the heartbreaking work day to day. Distancing oneself from traumatic impact requires an unending supply of energy... yet for those caught in the middle, they may feel unable to do so. I know during my own phase, I learnedly always allowed financial difficulties and sociocultural realities to just be, because as my counselor, Mr. Scott always said, "You have to work at finding you." It may be endlessly tiring for you and/or your survivor to hear or speak of ideas in elementary phrasings. Let me tell you though, that the complexity and severity of a brain injury must be upheld or your survivor may remain lost on the TABIÆS. No one wants such a stationary outcome for the survivor.

In 2016, I had the privilege of presenting a poster with Craniama to the World Congress of the International Brain Injury Association at The Hague in the Netherlands. I set out to explain a minor perturbation which I had written regarding a self-assessment tool known as the Wong-Baker FACES® Pain Rating Scale (FACES Scale). Ideas regarding my TABIÆS were still in their infancy and now that I have gained some feedback, this poster presentation has become a bonus chapter to the second edition.

The focus of the healthy patient's experience in the hospital setting is based on the ideological process of the body's work towards homeostasis. Some might argue that the duty of medical staff is primarily to soothe

the inadvertent humiliation of doctors' prognosis, directives, treatments, and prescriptions. It is known that the grandmothers said: "the doctor is the father, the mother, the nurse and the patient, the child." The memory also stated that the child (well, for this comparison, the patient) should speak only when spoken to.

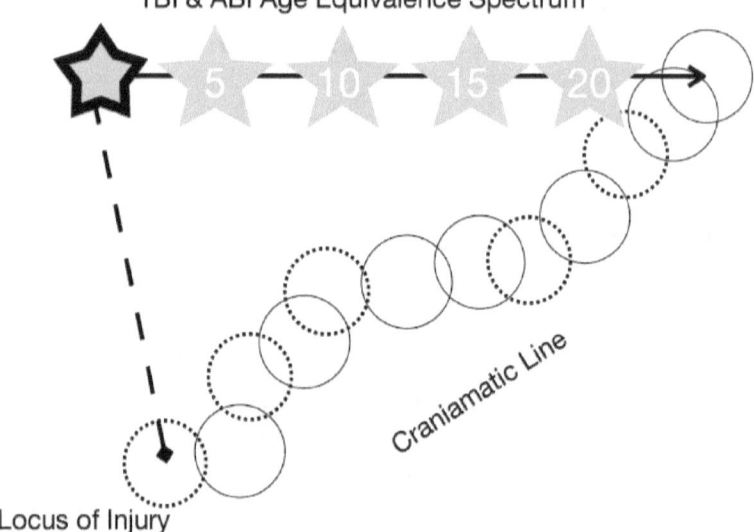

The Traumatic & Acquired Brain Injury Age-Equivalence Spectrum, a reference in the paradigm of survival as pictured above. The TABIÆS is a place plotting diagram designed for the second ascent to adulthood following trauma that begins as shown with a falling star (loss of consciousness in the locus of injury). Such a graphic is intended to help the struggling patient perceive the brain recalling their own memories (shadow-self) while recalibrating the spirit (mind) through the process of recovery to match again with their grown heart (body and soul).

At the World Congress on Head Injuries, I do not know if she was a doctor or not, but the mother of a severely brain injured patient approached the path where my poster was. "Thank you for that," she said. "My thirteen-year-old daughter could not speak for about a year and every time they presented the face scales, she pointed to the happiest face. It was not until she started talking that we finally understood what she was talking about. Then we found out that she chooses her face because she was wishing to be gentle and transparent instead of confessing her pain."

When starting a new TABIÆS, people with acquired disabilities may not have the natural ability to understand the processes of human physiology and behavior. For the patient struggling to survive a head injury, he/she sometimes seems unintelligible or confused. Be careful not to apply methods of caring for family members with dementia, as the brain-injured person will still have full understanding unbreakable, but will still choose to allow other people's thoughts to define the situation. In my opinion, such ideas can be intentional, and at other times unintentional.

The ability of survivors to achieve social success should not be seen solely as their responsibility - at a minimum - during the first five years of recovery. These 10-15 or 20 years of recovery, and sometimes longer, make up the nebulous new paradigm that I am introduced with the copyright of this book back in 2015... the age-equivalence spectrum of traumatic and acquired brain injuries (TABIÆS). This spectrum bases its continuum on a chart that allows the coma survivor to mark their beginning plot in tandem with caregivers focused on recording the progression of recovery during the future years following intense trauma.

As further independence comes about, the survivor can best begin to explore the TABIÆS that is currently being tested. Although other applications may be allowed or even conceived, TABIÆS is only known for anyone surviving unplanned physical changes after birth. The Wong-Baker Pain Scale discovering the facial expression is so fully integrated into the medical system that it is not my intention to replace or distort the uniqueness offered by hospitals and useful to so many everywhere.

Time spent in the TABIÆS ought not to be rushed for any reason. The internal pain recognition array is designed to cover the entire spectrum as if looking in front of the body. Sometimes in the young and severely injured, the impulse to identify a specific parabiosis is built instead of what the patient hopes to achieve, rather than indicating the degree of nociceptive suffering. According to the Wong Baker Foundation, every patient must be able to understand the FACES tool and be able to show which person best reflects their experience of pain. In heaven, I am sure that objective identification of pain can lead angels to care for them, but on earth, the ideology of suffering remains entirely subjective and may not always fit into the scale of the face table.

God is the only trustworthy person in this world.
Patience becomes the key to suffering.
But dear heart be quiet! Do not tell the secret.
Strangers cannot sense the secret of the mind.
But suffering past these words, patience detects the key.

— Rumi

FORTHWITH

At some point (it's different for each person), but somewhere, the road that is less traveled will call you. I can only tell you honestly about my experience during Covid-19's escape and I do not give instructions or advocate for my personal choices over listening to your medical professionals.

When my doctor told me it would take 20 years for me to fully recover as an adult, I was angry. Honestly, it seemed like the longest road and such an exhaustive path. When this book was first published in 2015, although it had many errors and vague metaphors, I proudly thought I had achieved the goal of recovery. What I chose not to explain at such a time, was that I still needed a full range of pain medications. My headaches were quite severe and although I tried several times to get rid of them, the pain was too excessive that the idea of going without was inconceivable.

In July 2020, I do not know if I caught Covid or not, but for the next four months I was in some kind of cloudy headache fog, and on October 15, 2020 - twenty-one years before the day of the accident - while reading the Bible, I was surprisingly warm enough to develop perspiration on the sides of my forehead. This is my experience, not a woomera propelling some ad for the unseen. I felt like I was under a heat lamp. Then they warmed my lips as I closed the manuscript, and I was immediately cold and refreshed.

It took me almost seven years not to be addicted to prescriptions. It took me another year-and-a-half to complete the withdrawal. Now I take only vitamins, mineral supplements, and occasionally acetaminophen. I still have my allergies, but if I were asked to just give up while on the TABLÆS, I would still defend my right to take the same prescribed medication. No matter where you are at this point of reflection, your recovery must process with satisfaction following the tortoise. Ignore the spirit of the hare.

Help others understand that their work in restorative treatment does not happen in isolation. If any survivors are even familiar with suicidal ideation, a reminder that their trajectories are uniquely relevant should be allowed to develop with their lives. Depression and pain are so closely related that the pathway toward clarifying the physical brain is helpful because their attention may gain importance in the future teachings of the worldwide medical community. Suicide helplines are easily accessible via search engines on the Internet. Please remember: listen to your doctor, take your medications as prescribed, work hard every day without giving up… control yourself and always claim patience within.

As you eventually leave this book on the shelf, don't forget to consider all viewpoints peacefully and wait expectantly for understanding. Everyone makes mistakes in a free society. Not one survivor is perfect. Emotion does not edify knowledge. The restitution performed by Social Justice, much like her sister Survival, is not a step-by-step list for some kanban system…, because interpretation hides in a wheel of ever-changing ideals. Persuasions are not independent of ideology, but rather dependent upon the opportunity for thought.

Though the ascension of surviving never really attains any singularity of survivor-hood, the purpose of your recovery awaits determination in the house of survival. In order to taste the fruits that truly impart personal inspiration, one desiring to survive must sow the proper seeds. When planted in the mind, irrigate with faith. Follow the process now, and then wait for the flourishing hope which eventually bears endurance. Champion patience caring for your shadow-self. As you near sunrise with recovery, the flower of your life will blossom…, filling at last, the innermost piece of the puzzle that leads to the wisdom of being alive.

Go forth with Godspeed sharing recent knowledge of your own mindedness. Best wishes with your journey through the TABLÆS.

APPENDIX 1

EMERGENCY TRAUMA PROTOCOL

This is included so those impacted by brain injury might be aware of the legal procedures happening at the onset of trauma. The purpose of this protocol is to outline the general approach to the patient with a traumatic injury.

Scene Size-Up

- Assure that the scene is safe for you, other rescuers and the patient. It may be appropriate to withdraw from the scene in some situations until a safer environment can be obtained. Or it may be appropriate to rapidly extricate the patient from a dangerous situation.
- Identify the number of patients and other resources that may be needed
- Initiate the Incident Management System if appropriate
- Call for law enforcement and/or first responder assistance if needed
- Call for additional EMS reinforcements as needed
- Begin triage if appropriate
- Identify yourself and seek permission to examine and treat the patient

Body Substance Isolation:

- Apply universal precautions / body substance isolation as appropriate Primary Survey
- Search for immediate life threats by assessing the patient using C-A-B process (circulation survey and controlling external hemorrhage, airway, and breathing) and treating the problems as they are found

Assessment

- Survey for any active external hemorrhaging.
- Assess airway with simultaneous cervical spine stabilization: Note patient's ability to speak, and any evidence of actual or potential airway obstruction including vomitus, bleeding, dentures, loose teeth or foreign anti-bodies.
- Assess breathing: Note patient's ability to speak, rate, depth and quality of ventilations, abnormal noises/stridor, retractions, accessory muscle use, nasal flaring, or cyanosis
- Assess circulation: Note the subject's pulse, level of consciousness, and identify any skin abnormalities (color, temperature, capillary refill, moisture)
- Assess neurological functioning (disability): Note the subject's level of consciousness, Glasgow Coma Scale or AVPU Scale, movement of each extremity

Intervention

- If major bleeding is present, control with sterile dressing and direct pressure. In the rare instance when direct pressure fails to control bleeding and the patient may exsanguinate, apply tourniquet(s) as appropriate or consider application of approved hemostatic dressing(s):
- Consider application of approved tourniquet(s) to control extremity hemorrhage per Application of Tourniquet Protocol
- Consider application of approved hemostatic dressing(s) to wounds in area(s) or that could not be controlled by placement of tourniquet per Use of Hemostatic Dressings Protocol

Secure Airway (While stabilizing the cervical spine with in-line restriction. Do not apply traction)

- BLS Maneuvers
- Jaw thrust, (head tilt - chin lift only if no concern about cervical spine injury)
- Oral or nasal airway
- Suction
- Assist ventilations with 100% oxygen and BVM if indicated by respiratory rate
- ALS Maneuvers
- Oral endotracheal intubation
- Orotracheal intubation may be attempted if unable to adequately ventilate the patient with BVM because of severe facial trauma or excessive blood or secretions. Maintain in-line cervical spine stabilization during attempts
- Transport of the unstable trauma patient should not be delayed by attempts at intubation unless the patient cannot be adequately ventilated with BVM
- Nasal endotracheal intubation
- Needle cricothyroidotomy

Administer oxygen

- Nasal cannula at 2.5 liters per minute oxygen flow
- Non-rebreather mask at 15 liters/minute oxygen flow
- Goal is to maintain SAO2 at a level greater than 97%

Assist ventilation as required

- Bag-valve-mask ventilation
- Bag to endotracheal tube ventilation

Assist circulation as required

- If no pulse is apparent:
- Follow DOA protocol if applicable

- Acardiopulmonary-arrest is secondary to trauma cannot be adequately resuscitated in the field and must reach definitive care without delays for any measurable possibility of survival
- Initiate CPR if indicated by circumstance
- Transporting of the unstable patient ought not be delayed in order to initiate IV therapy. Begin IV en route to the hospital. Introduce one or two large bore IVs with LR
- Administer fluids as per shock protocol
- Spinal restriction as indicated
- Maintain body temperature with blankets

Additional Notes

- Generally, minor abnormalities found in the primary survey are addressed most appropriately at the time of discovery
- It may be appropriate to move directly from the primary survey to another protocol (i.e. cardiac arrest, respiratory distress, shock)
- Bag valve mask ventilation is indicated prior to attempts at endotracheal intubation

Secondary Survey

- A systematic medical history with physical examination, focused on the patient's complaints, searching for problems that may not be immediately life or limb threatening, but that may become so if addressed inappropriately

Assessment

- Obtain chief complaint
- Obtain "SAMPLE" history
- Symptoms (including pertinent positives and negatives)
- Any known allergies
- Medications
- Past medical history
- Last meal
- Events/Environment leading to this episode

- Obtain various vital signs including the following: pulse, MANUAL systolic and diastolic blood pressures, respiratory rate, and determine patient's perceived pain score (Palpated systolic blood pressure is not sufficient except under extreme conditions)
- Perform focused physical examination (this evaluation is dependent on the above history as well as findings from the primary survey and may be more or less detailed depending on the situation)
- Consider application of cardiac monitor (paramedic interpret)
- Consider application of pulse oximeter
- Consider application of NIBP cuff
- Consider obtaining rapid beside glucose determination
- Assessment summation: Consider information gathered in primary and secondary survey, determine an impression of the patient's primary problem and proceed to the appropriate treatment protocol

Interventions

Obtain repeat set of vital signs prior to transfer of care to receiving facility or whenever there is an observed change in the patients status.

- Secure airway (see primary survey)
- Administer oxygen and assist ventilation as required (see primary survey) Consider establishing IV access en route to the hospital unless immediate transport is unavailable
- Consider administering drug therapies (as indicated)
- Right patient?
- Right drug?
- Right dose?
- Right route?
- Right time?
- Right reason?
- Right documentation?
- Allergies?
- The paramedic must read back to the assisting medical professional the above "Rights of the Medication Administration"
- Consider other therapeutic modalities (if indicated)

- Transport while monitoring vital signs and maintaining patient's comfort
- Decide the patient destination as determined by appropriate protocol
- Medical control contact as determined by appropriate protocol
Documentation:
- Document all assessments, vital signs, monitor findings, and interventions Considerations for Specific Body Areas

Assessment

- Head Trauma
- A - 1
- A - 2

As per primary and secondary survey - obtain patient's medical history in brief, noting mechanism of injury, use of safety devices and identify the level of present consciousness.

- Be alert for associated injuries.

Complete Intervention Procedures

- I - 1
- I - 2
- I - 3
- I - 4

As per primary and secondary surveys

- If intubation is indicated, administer lidocaine®, 1 mg/kg prior to intubation to help control intracranial pressure and administration of midazolam (Versed) 2.5mg IV if systolic blood pressure greater than 100mmHg for sedation.
- Administer IV fluids to maintain systolic blood pressure >120mmHg en route to hospital for severe head injuries with Glasgow Coma Scales of less than 9, otherwise titrate IV LR to maintain systolic blood pressure => 90mmHg.
- Transport as above

APPENDIX 2

WIELDING TABIÆS PRESENTATION #0022
by Bryan Sisson of USA

This summary is from the poster presented to the delegates attending the International Congress of Head Injury. The following excerpt was printed in the Oxford Journal. Such was my understanding at the time of 3/4 recovery. Now however, it will serve the reader better to refer to the dictionary and the edited materials, including the additional 17th chapter on the TABIÆS.

Abstract

On 16 Oct 1999, I was thrown from the backseat of a 15-passenger van. I became unconscious in the median, roughly 50 yards from where the van finally rested. Due to the severity of my skull fractures, broken bones and head injury, I remained in a coma for 15 days. Since returning home 23 Dec 1999, I have maintained idiographically valid observations of my personal experience. Anthropology seeks to give voice to the voiceless, which is my purpose for developing Craniama, while understanding my lens of recovery as the TBI & ABI Age Equivalence Spectrum (TABIÆS). Usage of the TABIÆS ought be integrated by survivors in later phases of their rehabilitation. Although, its my opinion that the realm of sociocultural discourse should be experienced before survivors begin to assess themselves in real time. Several benefits lie within this plot-style graph, which helps the survivor of severe head trauma plot their failures and successes along what I have termed, "the craniamatic line" (CL). All the while, a second line runs above in tandem with the CL, which appropriates any realized distance from whom a survivor would be/might have become absent severe head trauma. As a result of our highly mobile society, sickness and recovery are no longer borne in vacuous isolation in the home of a distant relative with a maximum of two or three physicians. In such a vacuous scenario: the patient, the caretaker, the physician, the neighbor, the colleague, the friend, etc. are each intimately acquainted with the plight, health and history of the one surviving. To be sure, recovery from severe head trauma will not eventuate successfully in isolation. TABIÆS garners the plausible outcome of helping medical professionals recreate the qualitative essence of the vacuum scenario despite sociocultural change in mobility, character, position and the survivor's acquired homeostasis. Additionally, a survivor's hopes, talents and their unique plans possessed pre-trauma can be discussed in specific detail with counseling professionals and those within the medical community. It has been my personal experience that when filling out continuation patient forms using the 1-10 emotional scale, a void persisted in not being able to express why I chose a specific number on a given day, which in hindsight, {ultimately} led to loneliness. I believe that patient-client satisfaction and understanding can be deepened drastically through the simple addition of TABIÆS. The concept for TABIÆS has been introduced in the book, Craniama: An Ethnography in Survival (© 2015 by Bryan Sisson).

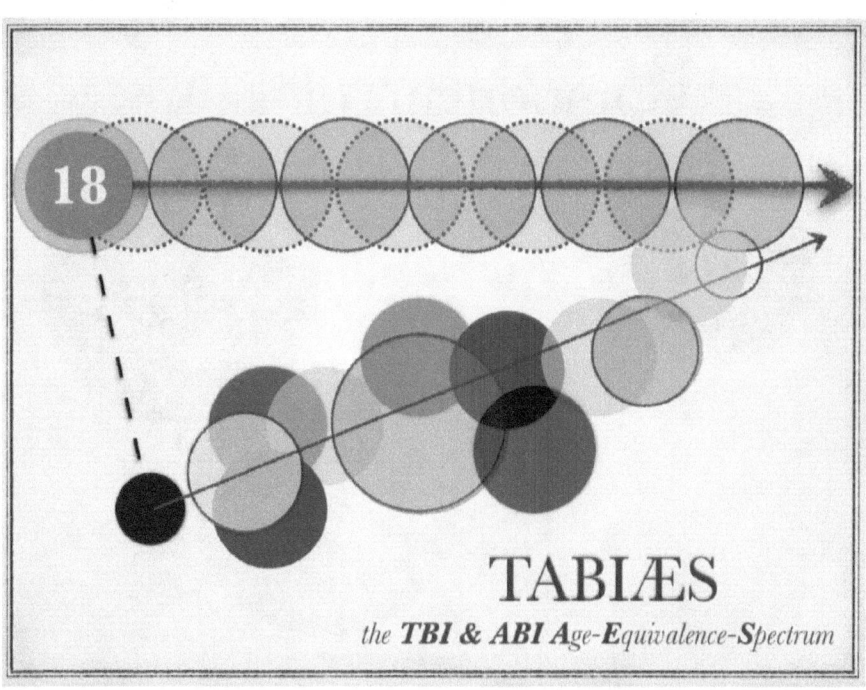

TABIÆS
*the **TBI** & **ABI** A*ge-*E*quivalence-*S*pectrum

Paradigm Postulate or Precept?

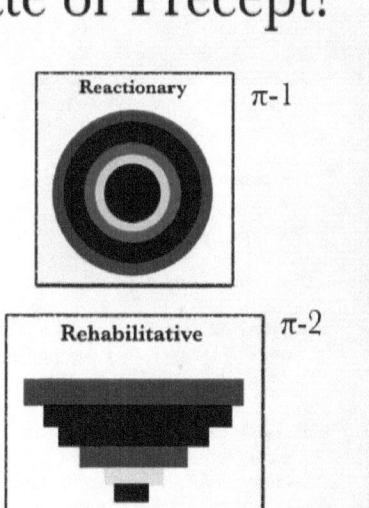

- 67% say when alleviating pain they're at the center of $\pi 1$ • 100% say when experiencing pain its at the bottom of $\pi 2$

- *Significant Conclusions*:

  - 97% of Physician's & medical personnel think of a patient in pain as $\pi 1$

  - 83% of survivor's conceptualize the doctor-patient relationship as $\pi 2$

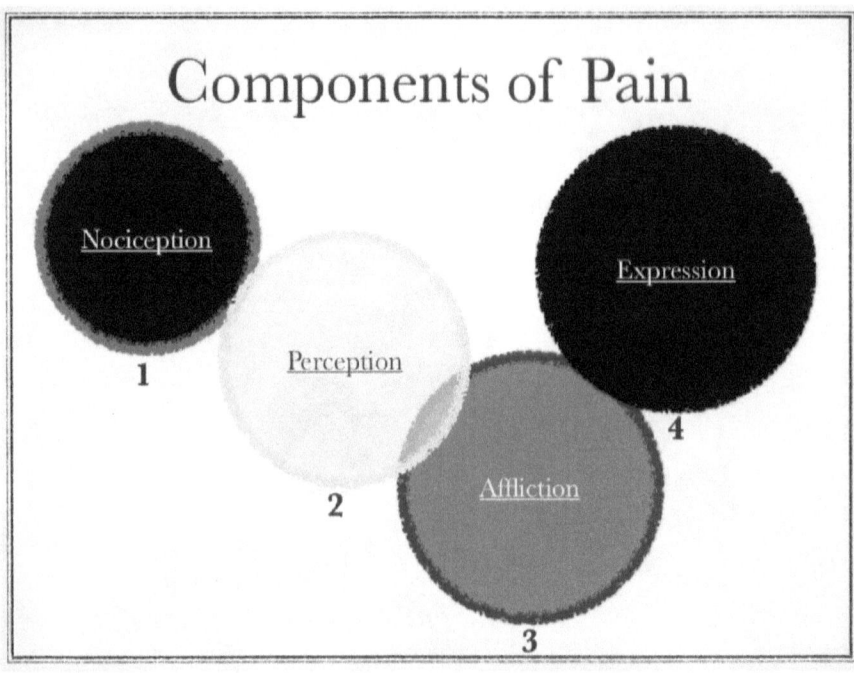

Components of *Physical Pain*

- **Nociception**: detection of tissue damage by specialized transducers attached to A delta and C fibers. While aspirin can prevent inflammation, remember that local and regional anesthesia can prevent nociception.

- **Perception**: Pain is triggered by a series of noxious stimuli. Realized pain can be generated by lesion in the peripheral or central nervous system, due to diabetic neuropathy, spinal cord injury and/or stroke. While pain can occur without nociception, the intensity of chronic pain has no relation to the extent of tissue injury or other pathology.

- **Affliction**: negative responses induced by pain and by fear, anxiety, stress, loss of loved objects and other psychological states. Cassell: *"Suffering occurs when the physical and psychological integrity of the person is threatened."*

- **Pain Behaviors**: resulting behaviors from pain and suffering and the things the person might do or does not do. Examples: *"ouch,"* grimacing, limping, lying down, recourse to health care, refusing to work, etc.

Archetypes OR Intelligences

Persona • a person's public personality, aspects of oneself that each reveals to others.

Shadow • prehistoric fear of wild animals, represents animal side of human nature.

Anima • feminine archetype in men.

Animus • masculine archetype in women.

Others • God, Hero, Nurturing Mother, Wise Old Man, Wicked Witch, Devil, Powerful Father.

Carl Jung

Sisson Pre-TBI • **ESTP**

Social Intelligence • the know-how involved in comprehending social situations and managing oneself successfully

Emotional Intelligence • ability to perceive, express, understand, and regulate emotions. "The EIQ involves the abilities to perceive, appraise, and express emotion; to access *and/or* generate feelings when they facilitate thought; to understand emotion and emotional knowledge; and to regulate emotions [*in as much as they may*] promote emotional and intellectual growth."

Mayer & Salovey

Sisson Post-TBI • **INTJ**

Defining Subjectivity

Features	Acute	Chronic	Traumatic
Etiology	Generally Known	Generally Unknown	*Exact*
Duration	Short, well characterized	Persistent post-healing	*Unknown*
Remedial Approach	Underlying disease	Underlying disorder	*Pervading Exactness*
TBIÆS	*Possibility*	*Plausibility*	

Survivors' Remorse

- Pain is defined by the individual.

- Pain is **totally subjective.**

- With TBI, survivors may not verbalize their pain but the tension always manifests in some visible way.

- With TBI, survivors often have varied sources of pain simultaneously.

- With survival from TBI, the individual becomes defined by society.

- Pain modulates toward objectivity.

Gardner's 7 Intelligences (1983)

1. **Logical**
2. **Linguistic**
3. **Musical**
4. **Spatial**
5. **Kinesthetic**
6. **Interpersonal**
7. **Intrapersonal**

GLOSSARY

THE A-Z OF TBI

Many, not all, of the symptoms described within this glossary shouldn't be viewed as consistent realities, but more like persistent possibilities that can happen at any given time during the 10-15 years along the TABLÆS. They even manifest after total recovery sometimes.

Waiting Room Glossary

1. **Acquired Brain Injury** (ABI) a traumatic event occurring post-birth; the injury is not hereditary, congenital, or degenerative; since ABIs occur on a cellular level, many cells in different areas may be affected as opposed to isolated areas of impact; it's opposite is the Congenital Brain Injury (CBI).
2. **Affect** (*flattened*) a perpetual paradigm lacking emotionality; a person can appear incredibly listless.
3. **Age-Equivalence Spectrum** see TABLÆS, a method of self-identification within the first 10-20 years following the initial impact of a survivor's brain injury. This graph easily summarizes achieved age or educational/socioeconomic status, etc. prior to experienced trauma. When working memory reengages at some point after the injury, the TABLÆS (tabaɪps) allows for survivors to choose exactly where they personally feel most comfortable at any given time. This may help medical professionals dissolve the current "lumping" of survivors into groups based on x-number of days, weeks or years since the traumatic onset.

4. **Agitation** a biological state of uneasy, restless and uncontrollable activity such as pacing, crying or laughing always possible at any time without apparent social reason.
5. **Agnosia** inability to recognize objects, expressions or traits that otherwise prior to the injury were automatically recognized.
6. **Agraphia** inability to write down or repeat something heard recently.
7. **Alexia** an inability to read, to which many medical communities sometimes refer, using its more commonly remembered title: acquired dyslexia.
8. **Alexithymia** the inability to recognize the connections between emotions can appear as alexithymia, a brain disorder that prevents understanding or expressing emotions. There is an emphasis on rationality but not a lack of desire for interaction. Research shows that this issue could be caused by an overactive left hemisphere, an underactive right hemisphere or simply poor communication between the two brain halves.
9. **Amygdala** the portion of the brain that modulates personal fears, while being responsible for a person's ability to read someone else's face for clues to read or sense how others may be feeling. Be careful though, if someone has facial nerve damage, you cannot read them in the same way as you would the rest of your acquaintances.
10. **Anarthria** severe dysarthria resulting in speechlessness. See dysarthria.
11. **Aneurysm** a mass in the wall of a blood vessel with a balloon like shape; as it grows, the wall surrounding it weakens which may lead it to burst resulting in a hemorrhage.
12. **Anomia** an inability to recognize or articulate names of objects or ideas as a result of brain trauma. This is commonly referred to as "tip-of-the-tongue" syndrome. Although offensive, this syndrome can at times be referred to colloquially as cerebral constipation.
13. **Aphasia** complete and total inability to communicate, although broken down into expression and comprehension.
    1. *Broca's* difficulty manifesting spontaneous speech.
    2. *Wernicke's* difficulty comprehending spoken words.

14. **Aphemia** an inability to verbally and/or physically express emotions or ideas in tandem with experience, although the survivor may likely exhibit success in writing and/or typing out what they are thinking.
15. **Aprosodia** neurological condition characterized by an inability to properly convey or interpret emotional prosody simultaneously and subconsciously in social discourse.
16. **Apraxia** the brain's subsequent loss of willed mobilizations, even though the impetus for performing said action is conceived in the mind.
17. **Asphyxia** a lack of oxygen or excess of carbon dioxide in the body, usually caused by physiological blocking and interruption of breathing, which causes unconsciousness: see suffocation.
18. **Ataxia** a problem with coordinating muscle movements due to the presence of a lesion to the cerebellum or basal ganglia. While the physiological placement interferes with a person's ability to walk, talk, eat and to perform other self care tasks, remember that this issue is not due to apraxia, weakness, rigidity, spasticity or sensory loss; even though the reality of these issues may be present.
19. **Atrophy** a state of wasting away or diminution. Muscular atrophy is often a visible decrease in muscle mass directly influenced by a survivor's time in the hospital. Diminution outside the hospital can at times be related to psychosocial factors including depressive symptoms.
20. **Autonomic Nervous System** (ANS) the part of the nervous system that controls involuntary activities, including but not limited to, a person's organs; this "part" is divided into 1) *sympathetic* and 2) *parasympathetic* systems (commonly referred to as fight or flight).
21. **Birth** the starting point of all characteristics and personalities.
    1. *Primary* every human experiences their primary birth; most often associated with a birthday and celebrated by family, friends, coworkers, etc. Special dinners, treats and birthday presents are often associated with the celebration.
    2. *Secondary* every survivor potentially experiences the second birth, most often associated with an anniversary that is

remembered privately. It is likely that others will not take interest in celebrating this achievement with you because they don't understand.
22. **Blood Brain Barrier** (BBB) employed by the brain for keeping unwanted objects/chemicals from entering the dura matter. The barrier has a tendency to malfunction in times of duress caused by hypertension, radiation exposure, infectious cells, and of course, brain trauma.
23. **Brainstem** the lower part of the brain that connects to the spinal cord. Functions located in the brainstem include those necessary for survival (breathing, heart rate) and arousal (being awake and alert).
    a. Difficulty sustaining breath and dependence on mechanical ventilation
    b. Dysphalgia
    c. Balance/movement problems
    d. Vertigo
    e. Sleeping issues
24. **Capism** a politically incorrect hierarchical evaluation of disabilities and those exhibiting signs, symptoms, etc. May also refer to the "I've been there," perspective initiated by self-help psychology based on philosophical perspectography and very little actualized theories.
25. **Central Nervous System** (*CNS*)- the nervous system proper, composed of the brain and spinal cord.
26. **Cerebellum** portion of brain coordinating commanded movement(s).
    A. Responsible for the coordination of fine movements and other examples of hand-eye coordination.
    B. Inability to walk and/or stand
    C. Tremors
    D. Vertigo
    E. Inability to change directions in rapid (or common) succession
    F. Slurred speech
27. **Closed-Head-Injury** head trauma where the skull remains unopened. It's opposite is the **Opened-Head-Injury**.

28. **Concussion** a violent non-penetrating injury to the brain; often accompanied by loss of consciousness.
29. **Congenital Brain Injury** *(CBI)* a brain injury most often introduced from conception or during delivery that can involve time spent in loss of consciousness following the first birth. It's opposite classification is the Aquired Brain Injury (*ABI*).
30. **Cortex** the outermost layer of the brain. Scientists estimate that this layer is the true seat of an individual's intelligence.
31. **Craniama,** *craniamatic* stems from Latin terms crani- meaning head with -iama meaning remedy. The concept encompassing the ten to twenty year-long paradigm of recovery spent within the TABIÆS; i.e. the amount of time encumbered for matching the internal personality with the outward appearance of the survivor's acquired personality. As this is unique to every individual, the craniamatic line is also exclusive to each person.
32. **Craniotomy** a procedure that involves the removal of a portion of the skull to expose the brain.
33. **Déjà-vu** an inexplicable sense of familiarity that causes individuals to believe they have heard, seen or experienced something before although certainty sustains the current experience is new.
34. **Delirium** typically develops over two to three days. Early clinical manifestations include difficulty in concentrating, restlessness, irritability, insomnia, and poor appetite. Some persons can experience seizures as a result. Unpleasant, even terrifying, dreams may occur during sleep.
35. **Dementia** essential features of the survivor's paradigm in a state of Dementia Due to Head Trauma (DDHT) is the observable presence of dementia judged to be caused by the direct pathophysiological consequences resulting from head trauma. The severity and type of cognitive impairments or behavioral disturbances manifested depends on the trauma location and extent of the survivor's brain injury. Posttraumatic amnesia is frequent, along with a deficit in persistent memory impairment. A variety of other behavioral symptoms may present themselves in the survivor, with or without any observable presence of motor or

sensory deficits. These symptoms can include, but are not limited to: aphasia, attentional problems, irritability, anxiety, depression or affective lability, apathy, increased aggression, or various changes in personality. Alcohol and/or Substance Intoxication is often present in individuals with acute head injuries. Concurrent Substance Abuse and/or Chemical Dependencies may persist along the TABIÆS trajectory. These superimposing effects can be emotionally taxing on survivors causing additional issues including, but not limited to: instances of hydrocephalus and/or Major Depressive Episodes (294.1 DSM-5 2014).

36. **Dementia Pugilistica** progressive dementia which is often the result of multiple and/or repeated brain injuries.
37. **Dendrite** these fibers extend from nerve cell (neurons) serving as data receptors for electrochemical impulses.
38. **Diabetes Insipidus** a unique condition caused by a ruptured or displaced hypothalamus resulting in survivors perceiving some confusing inability to quench their thirst. This symptom can manifest during moments of stress or anxiety, when the survivor is hydrated and very often manifests while drinking chilled water or cold Gatorade. (Not to be confused with dry mouth or "cotton mouth," as some refer, which is the result of multiple medications).
39. **Diminution** reduction or lessening.
40. **Dipoplia** condition in which a survivor can't focus their eyesight and exhibits double vision.
41. **Dysarthria** clinical term for "slurred speech," most often accompanied by tiredness and confusion during moderate to severe headaches; research has shown that this condition worsens over time if left uncorrected.
42. **Dyslexia** impaired ability learning to recognize shapes and symbols.
43. **Dysphagia** impaired difficulty with swallowing.
44. **Dysphasia** impaired ability to communicate.
45. **Dysomnia** inability to sleep properly.
46. **Dyspnea** extreme shortness of breath, referred to by some professionals as an experience in "air-hunger".
47. **Echopraxia** an involuntary repetition of another person's actions.

48. **Echolalia** an involuntary and repetitious production of sounds, syllables and/or words or phrases.
49. **Edema** an increase in retained water, which normally produces swelling.
50. **Emesis** experienced nausea and/or vomiting, usually referred to colloquially as tummy-ache, throwing-up and by some in even less savory terms.
51. **Emotion** a complex state-of-mind based on mental, physical and motor responses triggered by the survivor's perceived environment.
52. **Emotional Appropriateness** social correctness and suitable rendering of personal feelings as evaluated objectively.
53. **Emotional Blunting** the dulling of a survivor's emotional response.
54. **Emotional Lability** exhibiting rapid, sudden and drastic changes in emotional status inappropriately and without apparent reason. (happy, angry, sad, loving, kind, bitter, etc.) Survivors may feel they are correct in their judgement of social situations, but it should be remembered that while on the TABLÆS, the basis for their true emotions may be seen by others as "childish" or "immature".
55. **Emotional Need** a survivor's yearning for another person who is understanding, empathetic and supportive; exaggerated desire for one with whom they might share their emotional secrets. The problem with this natural conception of someone who exists to help the survivor wrestle with ideas and social in-appropriation is that at some point, the one supplying the survivor's emotional need may tire and be unnecessarily cruel because they perceive the emotional neediness exhibited by the survivor as high-school-ish and quite possibly, "immature". The solution to filling emotional need is that of emotional support.
56. **Emotional Support** a recognition and understanding that survivors ought to seek grounded, centered individuals who can offer respect and empathy for a survivor's reality as caught between two personalities. In certain social circles, those that offer the best emotional support to the survivor make-up the survivor's family-of-choice.

57. **Enoxaparin** a low-molecular-weight version of heparin that acts like heparin as an anticoagulant medication. Enoxaparin is used to prevent thromboembolic complications (blood clots that travel from their site of origin through the bloodstream to clog another vessel) and in the early treatment of blood clots in the lungs (pulmonary embolisms).
58. **Euphoria** any exaggerated or overwhelmingly abnormal sense of wellbeing that is not theorized or conceived in appropriate reality. Surprisingly, this is often relayed from others looking on the survivor and hastily estimating:
    a. Relax already, you look fine.
    b. I don't see anything wrong with you.
    c. You look 100% to me.
    d. You ruminate over the same issues so that you recreate self-fulfilling prophecies.
    e. Grow up already!
    f. I think you're over it now… let it go.
59. **Family-of-chance** any number of individuals that the survivor encounters while working through the TABLÆS. Time spent with the family-of-chance kindles the perceptibility of the survivor's ability to express her/him-self in some way that is remarkably different from that which was exhibited by the survivor's shadow-self.
60. **Family-of-choice** any number of friends, family members, mentors, professionals and at times, even co-workers that create a nucleus of supportive acceptance for survivors on the TABLÆS who are troubled by their new personality. These people do not necessarily have knowledge concerning brain injuries.
61. **Family-of-origin** the genetic ties of hereditary kinship and genealogical descent.
62. **Filter** lay terminology that describes an individual's ability to take in their surroundings and choose a socially compatible response.
63. **Frontal Lobe** the front portion of the human brain; emotional control system (ECS); involved in planning, organizing, problem solving, selective attention, personality and various "higher cognitive functions." Isolated difficulties present in injuries to this section of the brain can include, but are not limited to the following:

a. Paralysis
   b. Difficulty performing tasks in sequence
   c. Decreased spontaneity when engaging with others
   d. Inability to think flexibly
   e. Perseveration (a persistent single thought)
   f. Problems with ideological attendance (focusing on-task)
   g. Often surprising and seemingly odd quickened shifts in mood lability
   h. Sociological/behavioral changes
   i. Difference in overall personality type
   j. Decrease of ability to problem solve
   k. Broca's aphasia (difficulties verbally expressing language)
64. **Gloss Pharyngeal Breathing** (GPB) a means of forcing extra air into the lungs expanding the chest to achieve a functional cough. Referred to colloquially as "frog breathing."
65. **Grandiosity** boastfulness of one's character through bragging and/or self-praising.
66. **Hematoma** a localized collection of blood, usually clotted, in or near an organ, space or tissue, caused by a break in the wall of a blood vessel.
    A. *Epidural* outside the brain but underneath the skull.
    B. *Intra-cerebral* inside the brain tissue and/or dura matter.
    C. *Subdural* between the brain and its fibrous covering.
67. **Hallucination** false identification of an individual's perception(s).
68. **Hemiparesis** loss of controllable movement in one or more areas of the body. The loss can sometimes encourage something referred to as the, pusher syndrome. (See #94). Keep in mind that this hemiparesis is different from hemiplegia.
69. **Hydrocephalus** a build-up of cerebrospinal fluid between the brain and skull, which is one of a few symptoms that will result in changing a closed-head injury into an opened-head injury due to the shunt inserted just beneath the skull to rid the head of excess fluid.
70. **Hyperhidrosis** excessive and relentless sweating, often the result of little air movement, which can be exaggerated along with any injuries to the hypothalamus. It's common for non-professionals to evaluate excess sweat as being the result of

hormonal imbalances or anxiety with additional biological stresses.

71. **Hypothalamus** due to it's location as a dangling attachment to the brain with respect to the bowl that the brain rests on, it is possible for a rupture or additional fissure to develop when this bone becomes fractured and/or broken. The main job of the hypothalamus is to regulate the body's hydration levels.
72. **Glascow Coma Scale** Based on motor response, verbal performance, and eye opening to appropriate stimuli, the Glascow Coma Scale was designed and should be used to assess the depth and duration of coma and impaired consciousness. This scale helps to measure the impact of a wide range of conditions such as acute brain damage due to traumatic and / or vascular injury or infection, metabolic disorders (eg, hepatic or renal failure, hypoglycaemia, diabetic ketosis), etc.

The Glascow Paradox
Eye Opening Response
- Spontaneous--open with blinking at baseline 4 points
- To verbal stimuli, command, speech 3 points
- To pain only (not applied to face) 2 points
- No response 1 point

Verbal Response
- Oriented 5 points
- Confused conversation, but able to answer questions 4 points
- Inappropriate words 3 points
- Incomprehensible speech 2 points
- No response 1 point

Motor Response
- Obeys commands for movement 6 points
- Purposeful movement to painful stimulus 5 points
- Withdraws in response to pain 4 points
- Flexion in response to pain (decorticate posturing) 3 points
- Extension response in response to pain (decerebrate posturing) 2 points - No response 1 point

Categorizations of Comatose
- No eye-opening (scores less than 2)
- No ability to follow commands (scores less than 6)
- No word verbalizations (scores between 3-8)

Head Injury Classification
- Severe Head Injury (scores of 8 or less)
- Moderate Head Injury (scores between 9 and 12)
- Mild Head Injury (scores between 13 to 15

73. **Incomplete Head Injury** an injury leaving some loss of sensation or motor control below the spinal cord lesion.
74. **Jamais-vu** Understood in summary by the international Medical community as French for "never seen." (J'a'mais vous - literally, "I have never seen you.") familiar places, people, ideas and objects appear to be consciously foreign or unknown; see déjà-vu.
75. **Locus of Injury** locus is shown as a centralized TABIÆS concept. As an archeological excavation of the ancient layers, the locus (focal point in time) captures everything related to the moment of injury. Such a suspension separates us from the individual and we may feel as if the person we were was lost forever. But whenever the recovery process reaches a distance, the reality of survival allows the patient to develop the ideology of his or her original brain and see the physical effect as his or her shadow. The experience of the survivors can be understood as an innate functionality with or without awareness of their own shadow — I used this angle.
76. **The Los Rancheros Amigos Scale** (RLAS) also known as the Ranchos Scale, is a widely accepted medical scale used to describe the cognitive and behavioral patterns found in brain injury patients as they recover from injury.

Rancho Los Amigos Scale Parent/Survivor Paradigm

1. *No Response* Speak softly to the survivor, hold their hand, and tenderly massage the skin between their thumb and index finger. If you are religious or even questioning, pray.
2. *Generalized Response* Try not to let the TBI-patient see you become frustrated or cry. When they are able to

speak, listen intently and reassure them that everything is going to be alright.
3. *Localized Response* Show excitement for the things they are able to accomplish; like drawing a picture or successfully playing a free game of I Spy. If the patient misidentifies an object, don't laugh at them; but help them think of the right name.
4. *Confused or Agitated Response* Assure the TBI-patient that safety is sure. They can sometimes forget things you've explained recently, but if that happens, patiently explain to them what's happening and calm any fears they may have about being in the hospital.
5. *Confused, Inappropriate, Non-agitated Response* Not always the truth, but sometimes, the patient will return to your home and back to their bedroom with moderate independence. Don't be afraid to help them talk through ideas as they piece together memories of themselves. Start to fade out the classification of "patient," and begin incorporating language of success and survival. This will happen more naturally as the future survivor spends less attentional time in the hospital.
6. *Confused, Appropriate Response* Sit down with your new survivor and help them set realistic, small goals. Replace the original version of physical inadequacy with the hope of survival. Do what you can to help them carry out these tasks. Once success is accomplished, the process of accepting any acquired differences is realized and self-management naturally begins. Now the concepts of the TABLÆS and possibly this book should be incorporated into the surviving framework of forward understandings as they become increasingly aware of their new changes and personality type.

77. **Loss of Consciousness** (LOC) a full recovery foundation for establishing the first division of brain injury into three groups; including, a) if lasting less than six hours is generally referred to as a mild concussion, b) a moderate concussion between six and twenty, and c) anything longer than twenty hours, a severe brain injury.

78. **Major Head Injury** trauma to the brain resulting in some verifiable loss of consciousness.
79. **Memory** the ability for the human brain to remember, function and recall.
    A. Declarative the memory of learning
    B. Episodic the memory of episodes through which we associate time and space.
    C. Non-Declarative the unconscious "motor" memory of individual behaviors, habits, skills and outcomes.
    D. Implicit the unconscious memory of previous experience.
    E. Cerebellar the memory of non-motor functioning.
    F. Emotional mediated by the amygdala, which attaches positive or negative dispositions to various stimuli.
    G. Explicit conscious memory through which survivors intentionally recall previous experience and thought.
    H. Procedural the unconscious motor memory through which survivors recall how to: tie shoelaces, swim or ride a bike.
80. **Mental Status** the degree of competency to which an individual displays when given standardized tests used to determine overall intellectual, emotional, psychological and personality functions.
81. **Minor Head Injury** (mABI) trauma to the head resulting in little to no loss of consciousness.
82. **Occipital Lobe** the area responsible for visual processing; located in the posterior of the head. Isolated difficulties present in injuries to this section of the brain can include, but are not limited to the following:
    a. Persistent visual defects
    b. Difficulty finding objects in various settings
    c. Color agnosia (difficulty differentiating colors)
    d. Hallucinations
    e. Illusions (seeing objects inaccurately)
    f. Word Blindness
    g. Inability to recognize printed and/or drawn objects
    h. Movement agnosia (difficulty in recognizing an object's movement)
    i. Decreased ability in reading/writing

83. **Open Head Injury** trauma to the brain resulting in loss of consciousness due to the penetration of the brain.
84. **Osteitis** inflammation of bone tissue.
85. **Papilledema** a swelling of the optic disk which is part of the optic nerve, very often the primary symptom of hydrocephalus.
86. **Paralysis** defined as complete and total loss of strength of an affected limb or muscle group or body area.
    a. Monoplegia paralysis affecting only one limb
    b. Diplegia paralysis affecting the same body region on both sides of the body (both arms, for example, or both sides of the face)
    c. Hemiplegia paralysis affecting one side of the body
    d. Paraplegia paralysis affecting both legs and the trunk
    e. Quadriplegia paralysis affecting all four limbs and the trunk
87. **Parietal Lobes** areas of the brain that control spatial information (right lobe) and language (left lobe). Isolated difficulties present in injuries to this section of the brain can include, but are not limited to the following:
    a. Visual Attention Disorder (*VAD*) Inability to pay attention to more than one object simultaneously
    b. Anomia (inability to give an object its appropriate name)
    c. Agraphia (inability to find the appropriate words for writing)
    d. Alexia (difficulty reading)
    e. Constructional Apraxia difficulty drawing objects or assembling pieces to create shapes or structures
    f. Difficulty in distinguishing left from right
    g. Dyscalculia (difficulty in performing mathematical functions)
    h. Apraxia (lack of awareness of surrounding space or body parts)
    i. Blurred vision - an inability to focus
    j. Decreased hand/eye coordination
88. **Perseveration** the ability for survivors to subconsciously dwell on individual or groups of recurring thoughts persistently. My roommate always referred to this as "dwelling"...see RME.
89. **Photophobia** great discomfort or trepidation of bright lights. Just as various stimuli can produce side-effects during recovery, bright lights at times can contribute to pains attributed to areas "behind the eyes, inside the head".

90. **Prosody** the interpretative quality of expressing oneself subconsciously, using an audible range of vocal pitches in tandem with any number of rhythms through which human beings highlight stress and intonation for the purpose of conveying emotion.
    a. Prosodic Dysfunction some survivors may have problems with intonation, inflection and at times, appropriate volume.
91. **Prosopagnosia** a seldom occurring, but conscious inability to recognize faces of individuals from within the survivor's sphere of influence that would be otherwise identifiable.
92. **Post Concussion Syndrome (PCS)** a paradigm including impairments in the ability to think, act, and recall/re-learn information; characterized by unreliable memory, rapid mood swings, poor concentration, headache, dizziness, hypersensitivity, depression and anxiety. PCS is usually the aftermath of mild to moderate brain injuries.
93. **Patient** though hospital staff prefers us patienting, the one struggling to survive is really a client of the medical care system.
94. **Post-Traumatic Brain Injury Syndrome (PTBIS)** a set of symptoms experienced by survivors of ABIs.
95. **Shadow** according to Psychological words, such is the emersion into the darkest side of the individual personality. As the academy has not yet accepted the Cranial distance theorem which includes views not just simply positive and negative, recovery of the patient brain may not reflect the physical activity of the new human behavioral system which results indicated the new individual personality type.
96. **RME** Rolling my eyes.
97. **Spoonerism** transposition of initial consonants in any pair of words (see page 53).
98. **Shearing** microscopic lesions in the brain caused by the uncontrollable movement of the brain within the skull experiences straining on the delicate nerve fibers and blood vessels causing them to stretch above their normal capacities and rupture.
99. **Survivorship** the act of surviving is a life-long process of recognizing personal reality and not recovering original

acquisition of physical devisions. Though the patient may rightly be identified as a survivor of trauma on the horizontal of intention, the depth of human knowledge still encompasses profound application in the vertical of international wisdoms. S/he survived, we are surviving, therefore I know survival. Some of us can be survivalists, but the others, like those who are humble, they are still survivors.

100. **TABIÆS** the Traumatic & Acquired Brain Injury Age-Equivalence Spectrum — a place plotting diagram designed for the second ascent to adulthood following trauma that begins with a falling star (loss of consciousness). Originally intended to help the struggling patient perceive the recovery process of recalling their own memories (shadow-self) while recalibrating the spirit (mind) to match again with the grown heart (body and soul).

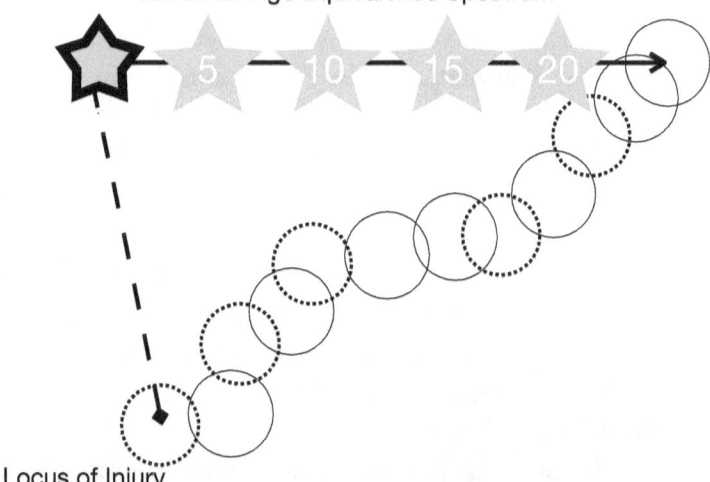

101. **Shunt** Cerebral when internal pressure inside the skull is abnormally high, a valve is placed under the skin to encourage the circulation of excess cerebrospinal fluid to other parts of the body.

102. **Synapse** the junction between a neuron and another neuron or muscle cell for transferring brain signals, sensory inputs, etc, throughout the nervous system.

103. **Syncope** the medical term for fainting. Presyncope is a state consisting of lightheadedness, muscular weakness, blurred vision, and feeling faint.
104. **Temporal Lobes** seat of the selective attention system (SAS); brain has two temporal lobes, one on each side of the head, at about the level of the ears. They are crucial to a person's ability of producing short term memory. They are also integral for two senses, both smell and hearing. Isolated difficulties present in injuries to this section of the brain can include, but are not limited to the following:
    a. Prosopagnosia (inability to recognize faces)
    b. Wernicke's aphasia (inability to comprehend spoken words)
    c. Difficulty recognizing objects
    d. Short term memory loss
    e. Difficulty remembering long term affects incurred via social interactions
    f. Increased/decreased sexual interests and/or behaviors
    g. Persistent talking (usually associated with damage to the right temporal lobe)
    h. Increased aggression
105. **Temporal Muscle** the muscle in the temporal region that operates movements of a person's jaw.
106. **Tetraplegia (Quadriplegia)** loss of functioning affecting all four limbs.
107. **Tracheostomy (Tracheotomy)** an incision into the lower neck area for the purpose of obtaining direct access to the windpipe as a means of controlling oxygen flow into the body.
108. **Trauma** injurious event caused by violent or disruptive actions.
109. **Traumatic Brain Injury (TBI)** an injury caused to the brain involving unconsciousness. These injuries can be broken into two main groups: opened-head and closed-head injuries. They are then further graded: either as minor, moderate or severe.
110. **Verbosity** an inability to express one's thoughts succinctly; needless wordiness.
111. **Whiplash** injury to the neck via violent back-and-forth, acceleration- deceleration movements of the survivor's head and

neck (such as in a rear-end car collision, falling from a rooftop or being tackled while jumping to catch a football). These injuries can cause substantial brain damage without directly injuring the skull.

112. **Withdrawal** a non-engaged, unsociable state perceived by non-traumatized as fear of life caused by any combination of apathy, lethargy, depression and introspection (*headinjury.com* 2014). The fact is that the above definition could be viewed as a form of 'capism. Survivors consciously understand the inability to engage on any identical level commiserate with our shadow selves while working through the TABLÆS.

113. **Word Blindness** a difficulty of survivors in recognizing words. Most often resulting from an injury to the occipital lobe.

WORKS CITED

THE BIBLIOGRAPHY

Internet Sites

1. http://www.anatomy-class.com/wp-content/uploads/2011/05/the-skull-I.jpg
2. http://www.telegraph.co.uk/news/religion/5144766/Most-peoplebelieve-in-life-after-death-study-finds.html
3. http://today.msnbc.msn.com/id/42191453/ns/todaytoday_people/t/meet-boy-who-says-he-visited-heaven-saw-jesus/
4. http://lwoodhealingarts.com/Shared_Worlds.doc
5. http://img.medscape.com/pi/emed/ckb/pediatrics_cardiac/906438-907111-626.jpg
6. http://www.neuroskills.com/brain-injury/traumatic-brain-injurystatistics.php
7. http://www.defense.gov/home/features/2012/0312_tbi/

Books, Journals & Articles

Abu-Akel, Ahmad (2003) "A Neurobiological Mapping of Theory of Mind," in *Brain Research News*, Vol 43. Printed by Elsevier Publications® in Los Angeles, CA.

Alexander, HB. (1912) "The Conception of 'Soul'," in *The Journal of Philosophy, Psychology and Scientific Methods*, Vol. 9, No. 16.

Baddeley, Alan D, Michael D Kopelman, Barbara A Wilson (2002) *The Handbook of Memory Disorders*, Second Edition. Published by John Wiley & Sons, Limited in West Sussex, England; UK.

Beales, David and Helen Whitten (2010) *Emotional Healing for Dummies*. Published by John Wiley and Sons, Limited in West Sussex, England; UK.

Bond, Frank W and Windy Dryden (2002) *A Handbook of Brief Cognitive Behavior Therapy*. Published by Wiley & Sons, Limited in San Francisco, CA; USA.

Brüne, Martin, Hedda Ribbert, Wulf Schiefenhövel, eds. (2003) *The Social Brain: Evolution & Pathology*. Published by John Wiley & Sons, Limited in New York, NY.

Calkins, Mary Whiton (1908) "Self and Soul," in *The Philosophical Review*, Vol. 17, No. 3.

Cook, Norman D (2002) *Tone of Voice and Mind: The Connections Between Intonation, Emotion, Cognition and Consciousness*. Published by John Benjamin's Publishing Company in Philadelphia, PN; USA.

Cummings, Benjamin (2007) Harvard Workshop covering *brain trauma etymology*. Copyright by Pearson Education, Inc.

Decety, Jean and William Ickes (2009) *The Social Neuroscience of Empathy*. Published by the Massachusets Institute of Technology in Cambridge, MA.

Denny-Brown, D (1943) "Factors of Importance in Head Injury," in *Virginia Law Review*, April, Vol. 29, #6, Law and Medicine Symposium.

Ekman, Paul (2003) *Emotions Revealed*. Published by Times Books, a Henry Holt and Company LLC.

Garrett, Brian (1998) *Personal Identity and Self-Consciousness*. Published by Routledge Publishers in London, England; UK.

Granacher, Robert P, Jr. (2008) *Traumatic Brain Injury: Methods for Clinical and Forensic Neuropsychiatric Assessment*, 2nd Edition. Published by the CRC Press of the Taylor and Francis Group in Boca Raton, FL; USA.

Green, Mark W, Leah M Green, and John F Rothrock, MDs. (2005) *Managing Your Headaches*, Second Edition. © by Mark Green, et al. Published by Springer Science + Business Media, Inc. in New York, NY; USA.

Harner, Michael. (1990) *The Way of the Shaman*, 3rd edition. © by Michael Harner and Published in San Francisco, CA.

Harris, Laurence and Michael Jenkins, eds. (2003) *Levels of Perception*. Published by Springer Publications in Toronto, Ontario; CA.

Heilman, Kenneth M (2005) *Creativity and the Brain*. Published by Psychology Press of the Taylor and Francis Group Publishers in New York, NY; USA.

Henry, Julie D, Louise H Phillips, John R Crawford, Magdalena Ietswaart, and Fiona Summers (2006) "Theory of Mind Following Traumatic Brain Injury: The Role of Emotion Recognition and Executive Dysfunction," in *Neuropsychologia*, Vol 44, pp 1623-1628. Published by Elsevier, Limited in the UK.

Herdegen, Timothy & J Delgado-Garcia (2004) *Brain Damage & Repair: From Molecular Research to Clinical Therapy*. Kluwer Academic Publishers in New York, New York with Copyright assigned to Springer Science + Business Media, Inc.

J Brandt, Magee WL, Dileo C, Wheeler BL, and McGilloway E. (2010) "Music Therapy for Acquired Brain Injury" (Review) in *The Chochrane Collaboration*. Published by John Wiley & Sons, Limited.

Kanz, Fabian and Karl Grossschmidt (2006) "Head Injuries and Roman Gladiators" in *Forensic Science International*. Vol 160. pp 207-216. Published by Elsevier Ireland, Limited Publications.

Kristiansen, Kristjana, Simon Vehmas and Tom Shakespeare (2009) *Arguing About Dissability: Philosophical Perspectives*. Published by Rutledge Publishers in London, England; UK.

Laird, James D (2007) *Feelings - The Perception of Self*. Published by Oxford University Press in New York, NY; USA.

Management, Progressive (2009) *Twenty-First Century War Veterans. Traumatic Brain Injury - TBI*. Copyright Progressive Management, Washington, DC; USA.

Okie, Susan, PhD (2005) "Traumatic Brain Injury in the War Zone" in *The NewEngland Journal of Medicine* Vol 352 (20) p2043.

Rahman, Barzan (2008) *An Applied Behaviour Analytic Approach to Challenging Behaviors Shown by Survivors of Traumatic Brain Injury*: a thesis submitted to the University of Birmingham for the Degree of Doctor of Philosophy. © by Barzan Rahman. Published by the School of Psychology at the University of Birmingham, England, UK.

Sala, Sergio Della, editor. (2010) *Forgetting: Current Issues in Memory*. Published by Psychology Press an imprint of the Taylor Francis Group in East Sussex, England, UK.

Schabracq, Marc J, Jacques AM Winnubst, Cary L Cooper (2003) *The Handbook of Work and Health Psychology*, Second Edition. Published by John Wiley and Sons, Limited in West Sussex, England, UK.

Scicutella, Angela, editor. (2007)

Seager, William (1999) *Theories of Consciousness; an Introduction and Assessment*. Published by Routledge Publishers in London, England; UK.

Shackelford, Ellen L. & Marguerite Edmonds. (2011) *Disability Etiquette Matters*. Copyright by Ellen L. Shackelford & Marguerite Edmonds. Printed by XLibris Publishers in Bloomington, IN; USA.

Skuk, Verena G. and Stefan R. Schweinberger (2013) "Adaptation Aftereffects in Vocal Emotion Perception Elicited by Expressive Faces and Voices," in *PLOSONE.com online journal*. © by the Departments for General Psychology and Cognitive Neuroscience in addition to the DFG Research Unit for Person Perception at the Institute of Psychology under the Friedrich Schiller University of Jena, Jena, Thuringia, Germany; EU. Published by *PLOSONE.com*.

Steckler, T; NH Kalin, and JMHM Reul, eds. (2005) *Handbook of Stress and the Brain: Part 2 - Integrative and Clinical Aspects*. © by T Steckler, et al. Published by Elsevier Publications in New York, NY; USA. Published by JSTOR.

Thilly, Frank (1912) "The Relation of Consciousness and Object to Sense- Perception," in *The Philosophical Review*, Vol. 21, No. 4.

Thompson, AH. (1889) "Facial Expression and It's Psychology," in *Transactions of the Annual Meetings*. Published by the Kansas Academy of Science. Vol. 12, pp. 67-74.

Vanderwolf, CH (2007) *The Evolving Brain: the Mind and the Neural Control of Behavior*. Printed by Springer Science + Business Media, LLC.

Wood, Lynn (2006) *Shared Worlds: A Thesis*. *http://lwoodhealingarts.com/Shared_Worlds.doc*, accessed June 18, 2011.

www.ingramcontent.com/pod-product-compliance
Lightning Source LLC
LaVergne TN
LVHW091545060526
838200LV00036B/709